Shhh...
Listening for God
Hearing the Sacred in the Silent

by
Cornelius W. May

Dr. Cornelius W. May
Faith Fellowship Church
10277 Valley View Rd.
Macedonia, OH 44056
(330) 467-1234
www.faithfellowship.org

Copyright © 2011 by Cornelius W. May

Shhh...Listening For God
by Cornelius W. May

Printed in the United States of America

ISBN 9781612155913

All rights reserved solely by the author. The author guarantees all contents are original and do not infringe upon the legal rights of any other person or work. No part of this book may be reproduced in any form without the permission of the author. The views expressed in this book are not necessarily those of the publisher.

Unless otherwise indicated, Bible quotations are taken from The New King James. Copyright © 1982 by Thomas Nelson, Inc. and The Message. Copyright © 1993, 1994, 1995, 1996, 2000, 2001, 2002 by The NavPress Publishing Group. Used by permisson. All rights reserved.

Cover Art by Neal W. May
Mount Sinai

www.xulonpress.com

May you meet Him
in the Stillness...
Dr. N. W. May

- Listening for God -

We need to find God, and He cannot be found in noise and restlessness. God is the friend of silence. See how nature... trees, flowers, grass grow in silence; see the stars, the moon and sun, how they move in silence... the more we receive in silent prayer, the more we can give in our active life... We need silence to be able to touch souls. The essential thing is not what we say, but what God says to us and through us. All our words will be useless unless they come from within. Words which do not give the light of Christ... Increase the darkness.

Mother Teresa

vi

TABLE OF CONTENTS

Acknowledgements ix

Foreword: Read this First xi

Prologue: Pathways to Presence xv

Introduction: If Silence is Golden xxiii

Chapter 1 – Cosmic Whisperer 27

Chapter 2 – Pickin' Up Good Vibrations 41

Chapter 3 – Hallowed Be Thy Time 57

Chapter 4 – Hear Ye, Hear Ye, Hear Ye 73

Chapter 5 – The Speaking Absence 85

Chapter 6 – Listening to Hear 99

Chapter 7 – Be Still and Know 111

Chapter 8 – From Private Silence to Public Shout 125

Chapter 9 – Quiet Places, Sacred Spaces 141

Chapter 10 – A Voice in the Wilderness 157

Chapter 11 – A Word from the Lord 173

Chapter 12 – Run Silent, Run Deep 185

Chapter 13 – The Silent Treatment 199

Epilogue: Do You Hear What I Hear? 211

Appendix 215

Bibliography 221

ACKNOWLEDGEMENTS

I've often heard that it takes a village to raise a child. And a book is no different. For those of us who attempt to be *"the pen of a ready writer"* (Psalm 45:1), the manuscript is very much like working through the stages of life. Along the way, special people are needed here and there. Authors need others to objectively reflect on style, thought, tenses, rhythm, clarity, syntax, flow, and Scriptural accuracy.

My church reading group, you know who you are, was monumental with meaningful chit chat and reciprocating banter of just how challenging listening for God can be. Yet, the autograph in hand stimulated a host of testimonial responses by those who are practicing hearing the Voice of God. Our times of gathering were most memorable. David and Karin, I appreciate your efforts revealed in the Discussion Questions.

Many others have read and re-read this work. Over and over again you were my sounding board. Each time I would say *"I'm finished,"* you greeted me with humorous remarks like *"Sure."* I've learned a book is a continuous outgrowth and may never end with a grand conclusion. Thought is constantly being stirred, as it should be. Thus, the story goes on. . .

Some names are mentioned throughout the work. Let this suffice as acclaim to your valued part in my life. Hosts of others have been greeted more personally for their sacrifice and friendship.

The list of associates and colleagues who continue to undergird my journey through brokenness with prayer and encouragement is too long to list individually. Thank you.

To my ministerial staff, Kathie, Jim, Mike and Joyce, please accept this mention as a deep gesture of appreciation for your heartfelt faithfulness (www.faithfellowship.org for more details of this illustrious team). You have lifted my arms when "things" got heavy and troublesome. Yes, we rise together to see another day. May God's grace be bountifully upon you all.

To my Church Board, you are a God-sent form of spiritual reliability. Remain strong and keep the faith.

And Ginger, whose title *"Secretary"* does not do her justice for the untold hours of unquestionable dedication, sincere prayer, and flexible willingness—you are an exceptional gift from Above to which you will receive eternal rewards.

God Bless,

Cornelius

Foreword

READ THIS FIRST

I don't know whether or not anybody has ever written a Foreword to their own book. I have a host of friends and colleagues to invite to write a Foreword who would do admirably and be much more articulate than my simple and sometimes circuitous thoughts.

I have admitted it publically, so it's no use trying to hide it here: I have significant levels of weirdness. Some of my *weirdnesses* have been healed; some are too exciting to give up. Just teasing. Maybe it was growing up in the 60s when creative thinking was encouraged and boundaries of limitation were dropped like hot potatoes.

A few words of clarification may assist with the entertainment value of this book. Entertainment is not sinful, although it can be, I guess. Entertainment is one of the acknowledged needs of any audience. People want to see or hear or read something good, or at least something that holds their interest, any something that deviates from the expected.

Have you found *"normal"* to be overrated? *"Normal is just a setting on a dryer,"* many admit. As a pastor for over three decades, I have noticed people strive to be normal and be like everybody else. What then? Bor-ing. Actually, none of us is really sure who set the bar for *"normal."* Where is it? How low or how elevated?

A well known brainiac of the sciences, Dr. Abraham Maslow, declares, *"What we call 'normal' in psychology is really a psycho-pathology of the average, so undramatic and so widely spread that we don't even notice it."*

I didn't want my book to be *normal*, that is, just another regurgitation of old discussions. So I elected to tell my story throughout. The ups and downs, the ins and outs, and the *"highs"* and lows.

My upbringing was greatly influenced by music. I played guitar. Early in life I veered from expected activities to learn an instrument. The Beatles had just arrived in America. The year? 1964.

Family dynamics were tested. My father had a butch haircut, a flat-top. Me? Long hair and fringed suede coats. Boots to match. You can imagine the family tension. My brothers were star athletes. Would I continue in the family line? Only if it's a bit winding.

Once upon a time, some 30 years after high school graduation, I walked into a store to order windows for my home. Lo and behold, behind the desk sat my former high school principal, Mr. Colonius. I couldn't believe it.

He didn't recognize me at first. I had to re-introduce myself to this acquaintance of by-gone years of tumultuous times. *"Mr.*

Colonius, it's me!" I said, *"Neal May."* With a look of horror, shock, and surprise all mixed into one, he gasped.

Then came the ultimate question I enjoy answering so often, *"What are you doing with yourself?"* With forthright confidence that bordered on spiritual pride, I exclaimed: *"I'm a pastor, a minister of the Gospel of Jesus Christ."*

This man of means, education, knowledge, and expertise extraordinaire leaned back with a slight push on his wheeled office like chair, threw both hands high into the air like a surrendering Pentecostal soldier, and jubilantly declared—*There is a God!!!*

I believe the Church would call my journey into the tempestuous dark and out into the glorious light, a testimony of God's grace. Who I once was is not who I am today.

Well, the rest of the story is told in the ensuing chapters. Scattered throughout are lines from songs, references to artists, or maybe a title now and then. Most are italicized. Musical melody is the cadence of the Cosmos. I hope you have some joyful discovery in the middle of a powerfully moving encounter with *"Listening for God."*

Prologue

PATHWAYS TO PRESENCE

In the midst of one of the greatest personal turmoils, my emotions were frayed, my spirit low. I was in pain inside and out. Ever been hit in the head with a baseball bat? I was experiencing severe migraine headaches in the back of my head everyday. Worst of all, God's Voice was barely audible, a faint tone off in the distance; even though I strained, I could not discern spiritual diction. I was alone.

When I needed God the most, God felt the farthest away. Was silence from the realm of Glory punishment for something I did? Maybe the Lord is a bit moody like the many gods of mythology. Or was the Kingdom of Light trying to draw me closer, teaching me to lean into Divine Presence?

Have you ever received a *"cold shoulder?"* Conflicts in life do arise and sometimes they are not diffused in the most mature of ways. But with God? I thought the *Great Physician* played by a different set of rules.

Ever feel like Heaven has closed its doors and bolted them shut? No amount of petitional ruckus can seemingly arouse a response. Like Dorothy and her friends knocking on the cathedral-type doors of Oz, you are just politely brushed aside. *"He's busy. Come back another day."*

If by chance I did recognize what I thought was God connecting, my intrapersonal struggle made me doubt what I had always known and trusted. In my clouded outlook, had I somehow distanced myself from God's loving care? What was I to do?

There is nothing like trouble in any form to set the distressed apart from the pack. In the disturbance of life's stormy seas, we discover who our true friends are and where others may stand. Some stand way in the back, far removed from our need of touchy-feely companionship.

But untold others, quite often previously unknown, step forward in support. Typically, they are persons who at one time or another have been deserted or abandoned themselves. These heroes of compassionate action have experienced the worst form of loneliness, the feeling of being alone in the midst of a crowd. Recording artist and friend, Lynda Rebecca Shaw, tearfully sings *"I felt alone, invisible and unknown."* To watch another individual endure such cruel isolationism is more than their awakened conscience can bear; and thus they commit to walk alongside.

To sympathize with another is to resonate with their distressing tones and vow to do something to alleviate their burden. Burden, *baros* in Greek, is where we derive our English word barometer. Barometers measure the heaviness of the air.

Some burdens are just too heavy for us to carry on our own. *The road is long with many a winding turn.* Vexed with strain, we need assistance for a time from someone like Simon the Cyrene to help carry our cross.

Historian, Ray Nichols observantly declares:

> The most beautiful of people I have known are those who have known defeat, known suffering, known struggle, known loss, and have found their way out of the depths.

> Those people have an appreciation, a sensitivity, and an understanding of life that fills them with compassion, gentleness, and a deep loving concern. . . Beautiful people do not just happen.

As a fractured vessel, I visited with a priestly man, Deacon Mahoney, an anointed therapist who gently penetrated the deepest of hurts and weighed my brokenness— *"He ain't heavy, he's my brother."* He listened to my spiritual dilemma and pointed me toward nature. *"Look for God's Voice in creation."* A new lesson, I had to learn to listen with my eyes.

God speaks in many ways, like through preaching, dreams, prayer, and nature. When we seem closed to one we can open to another. I believe it is usual for God to speak. We may not always hear what is being said; regardless, God is speaking.

My first walk outdoors was quite tranquil, but most episodic. I hiked to the top of the hilly terrain of southern Ohio at Camp

Shhh...Listening For God

McPherson. You may recognize the name. The property is held by the Four Square Church founded by Aimee Semple McPherson, former Pentecostal preacher. Truly the Spirit is in this place.

Arriving at a high level clearing, I discovered a barren swath that looked as though a large chainsaw had gone through and cut a breach wide and long. Recently a tornado had come across the crest and left in its wake total destruction. Branches and debris were everywhere.

Strolling through what was left of the once dense woodland, I felt like Nehemiah surveying the fractured walls of Jerusalem. As with prophetic eyes, I was amazed to find fresh green growth there, small shoots of future hope. Butterflies too! In the midst of the brokenness, God had spoken loudly into the void.

Nature abhors a vacuum and will fill it with newness when and where the old has been injuriously stripped away. God's messages in nature are frequent and multifaceted. Take a walk, look around, watch nature make a way past obstacles and through destruction. God continually creates; life finds a way.

I have seen trees grow around obstructions in fascinating curvatures. I have also seen them engulf a fairly large stone and use it as part of their structural strength. As Ralph Waldo Emerson concluded, *"All I have seen teaches me to trust the Creator for all I have not seen."*

Needless to say, God is bringing me through my ordeal, strengthening me as Paul would say *"with might by His Spirit in the inner man."* Though outwardly my situation continues to drag on through the muck and the mire, I am finding my path by concentrating on hearing God's Voice in new ways.

Ah, my book. Pastoring for over three decades in a strongly Pneumatic matrix (*Pneuma,* of course, is the Greek term for Spirit or wind) has been eventful to say the least. I have tasted and have seen the awesome goodness of God. But something is amiss. Silence has gone by the wayside.

One of the traits of the newly emerging religious scene is the pride of noise. Somehow we equate noise with the fullness of God. More noise, more power, more praise, more God; a very simple formula. Noise works rather well, it appeals to the senses; however, how Scriptural is it? Does it work spiritually?

If we look at the Old Testament architectural model of the Temple, there is an unfolding principle—***the closer we get to God the quieter it gets.*** Worshippers are to move from the noisy outer courts to the intimate noiseless Holy of Holies. C. S. Lewis, in *The Screwtape Letters*, called Hell the *"Kingdom of Noise."*

Arguments vary regarding the place of jubilant praise and more stoic atmospheres of reverential quietness. Most likely, we are to hold them in proper tension. The truth is usually in the middle. We'll see. Praise certainly *"stills the enemy,"* as the Psalmist states, but silence *"stills the soul."*

Divine intervention can be as elemental as invoking the Name of Jesus, He who is the Christ, Lord, and Son of God. Dealing with the ever so fragile human soul is a little more precarious. Like tending to sheep, we must tend to our soulistic needs or suffer the consequences of a life abounding with movement, but lacking direction.

So, I have decided not to overly fixate on pushing the alleged evil out of my situation or obsessively concentrate on calling the Angelic Hosts down upon it. Because at this time, none of my former methods of renewal and recovery like the laying on hands and anointing with oil, are bringing the joyful merriment of victory, which I and others relish so earnestly.

Wholeness is not always immediate. The *Great Physician* is called *"Great"* for a reason. God's ways are not always our ways. Faith makes things possible, not easy.

I have thus been forced to walk my journey of chronic pain and relational stress *"sacramentally"* by inviting the Good Shepherd to walk *"with me"* on the path of *the fellowship of His sufferings.* Either we walk together or I walk not at all. So now what?

From time to time you and I should quiet our beings through contemplative experience and center ourselves on Jesus who is the center of the Cosmos. In the quiet of the spiritual life, depth of soul is fathomed. Noise may seem like a short cut to constrain troubling inner disturbance, but it is unable to muffle what keeps rising to the surface.

Everything we repress has a way of coming out ugly. That is, it will unmask itself in dysfunctional conduct and performance. Insecurity, anxiety, eating too much or too little, anger, depression, compulsions, obsessions and a host of other neurotic tendencies may be displayed. Got ugly?

Shhh...Listening For God

Don't be afraid. God's delicate handling of our inner-wounds and filling the hole in the soul is just what the Doctor ordered. Søren Kierkegaard said that if he were a physician and were allowed to prescribe just one remedy for all the ills of the modern world, he would prescribe silence.

As with so many others, I continually find myself in the needy condition of requiring guidance. If I lack wisdom, James the Less, first Bishop of Jerusalem, simply says, *"ASK."* Nonetheless, it is hearing God's answer that is the problem.

I believe Scripture portrays us in a listening posture from the opening pages till the closing of the final chapter. In the animated words of Toonsville's greatest hunter, Elmer Fudd, we must learn to be *"vewy, vewy quiet."*

In what follows, we will explore the model exemplified in the lives of those seeking the Divine. Their frequent trips to places of quietude, and I add, often alone, bid us to come as well but for nothing more than to hear. Jesus always came away from such remote encounters with renewed strength and miraculous ability. Not bad. Not bad at all.

Together we will chart some of the Testamental pathways to God's Presence. Let's begin our journey, shall we? *Shhh*. God is speaking. . .

Introduction

IF SILENCE IS GOLDEN

If silence is golden why aren't more people pursuing this most precious commodity? When gold was first discovered, literally a massive migration occurred throughout America.

Traveling across rigorous landscapes, all types of people discarded their personal employments to go in search of that which promised a better life. Nothing could stop those in pursuit. Not distance, not setbacks, not hurts—nothing could keep the seekers from their illuminate goal—to find fortune. And many did.

Silence is the golden nugget of biblical spirituality. Like heading west, finding it will not be easy. But to lay claim to a place, a sacred place, a safe place, where the true riches are found, is to be genuinely celebrated. When it is found, like those digging in the mine, or panning for that first sight of sparkling glitter, joy overflows. Hard work has finally paid off.

I recall traveling in the Judean wilderness outside of Jerusalem and heading down to the Dead Sea. My first stopover was *En Gedi,* an oasis in the midst of nothingness. This is where David hid in the caves from Saul. The flowing rill musically cascaded in soothing abundance. *"As the deer pants for the water brooks so my soul pants after Thee."* Animals, trees, and plant life flourish.

Until that moment, there was only barren rock, sand, scrub brush, and wasteland. Then I saw it! Like a mirage appearing on the horizon. Were my blurry eyes and parched tongue deceiving me? No! Palm trees. Fruit. Precious life-giving liquid spilling forth. It was real!

To discover such a place overflowing with rejuvenating sweetness is the reward of pilgrimage. Once we have arrived and tasted of the experience, we will return again and again.

Several years ago, I had the fortunate opportunity of walking a vertical zigzag to the cramped peak of historic Mount Sinai in Egypt. It was an uphill climb all the way and not for the faint of heart. Our energetic tour group left base camp at two in the morning and finally arrived at the apex some three and a half hours later, just minutes before sunrise. Then we realized we must lumber back down, jolt by jolt, which actually took longer and was harder on the body.

Beginning the Mosaic ascent in the dark was the key to success. If we really could have seen how far we must go to perch ourselves on the edge of a rocky precipice, we would have never begun. But we did. We stepped into the constant flow of peoples and camels, torches and flashlights, which treaded the serpentine path to the summit.

From the bottom, it looked as if we were going to storm Frankenstein's castle. Shadowy figures tightly clenched luminous vessels and sojourned the poorly lit, stony trail, tracing the centuried steps of pilgrims past.

The memories of that occasion are forever recorded in my soul. To this day, I still testify that it was one of the most difficult things I've ever done, yet one of the best things I have ever done. As usual, they are related. I still am reaping rewards for my diligence and effort.

Likewise, the journey into silence is usually met with some resistance. Libraries are passé. Many of us have grown quite accustomed to the noisy world of modern day life. People read their paperless books in busy coffee shops. We are probably not even aware how clamorous life is until we attempt to quiet ourselves. Even when we have stilled our surroundings, our own mind kicks in thinking, scheming, conversing, planning, making it more difficult to just restfully sit.

No wonder Jesus said, *"go into your room [your closet] and shut the door."* Getting distractions out of the way is the initial step and will take intentional effort. Patriarch of Alexandria, Abba Agathon, put a stone in his mouth for three years to train himself in the discipline of holy silence.

I am writing these thoughts while staying at Mount Savior Monastery, which is situated upon a mountainous peak in western New York. The grounds are sacralized from years and years of prayer, offered seven times a day.

Mount Savior is a quiet place except for the bleating of the sheep, and the bray of a donkey at times (which keeps the *Wile E.* coyotes at bay). Other than church bells calling the retreatants to prayer, it is silent, sanctifyingly silent. It took several days to inwardly calm down and simply enjoy the Presence of God.

As a recovering, confessed workaholic, I found busyness to be an idolized addiction. The more I produced, the more my self-esteem was massaged; hence, the more accolades I was given and the better I felt. Truly masculine? Time will tell. Working all the time may be a good way to hide, but it is a very poor healer of the inner sanctum where wounds and hurts are deeply layered.

Imagine the jolt to my spiritual system. Being at a monastery is like slamming on the brakes after speeding along at 72 miles per hour. Only after a while, did I gently slide into the monastic rhythm and find inner peace and contentment. Wow. Then I heard the whisper of the Spirit, God's Voice in the wind and the ruffling of leaves. Long walks of solitude caressed my wearied soul.

Only in silence did I discover that I had been carrying heavy loads of care and concern. Busyness kept my true deteriorating condition from me. I was lulled into the false belief that I was doing fine. Carl Jung discerningly concluded, *"Hurry is not of the Devil; it is the Devil."*

How about you? How about me? Silence can and will be our best friend. Silence will inform. Silence will communicate more than we care to know. But silence will always convey all that we need to know. The Divine will meet us there. As we create the space, God will fill it. It is a spiritual principle. You and I need to position ourselves to hear.

Chapter One

COSMIC WHISPERER

I'm not sure who initially introduced the four journey model: the upward, inward, outward, forward view of life. I first heard it taught by Dr. Richard Parrot and Dr. Terry Wardle at the Pastors of Excellence Program hosted by the Sandberg Leadership Center in Ashland, Ohio.

This *cruciform* pattern [description mine] certainly explains the journey of faith in all its dimensions. In fact, the four dimensions can be easily recognized in the prayer of prayers, *"The Lord's Prayer."* These four facets of life and being capture all that we are and ever hope to be spiritually, emotionally, mentally, and relationally.

In my estimation, all parts of the journey model work best in a communal setting. We need others, no doubt. Ringo was right, *We get by with a little help from our friends.* Yet the inward piece is somewhat distinct. Though it is more individual in nature, a guide, a mentor, someone is needed who will take us by the hand to get us started.

All of us seem to face the same fear when it comes to looking within. It is the fear of feeling vulnerable, as when a blue-shirted, badged officer purposefully plucks the unsuspecting out of the slow shuffling line at airport security. Ever had a detection wand waived over, under, and around your entire torso? No Tinkerbell wish come true either. *Beep. Beep.*

We also know he or she is going to search every zippered compartment of our carefully packed matching pieces of designer luggage. Our secret inner life is about to be openly displayed on a shiny, stainless steel operating table.

Silence can have that same fearful affect. That's why many keep so busy, staying on the run. How's that working for us?

If the Devil cannot make us behave badly, he will let us busily behave. Needless to say, we cannot run fast enough or far enough to get away from ourselves. Everywhere we go, there we are. Geographical cures are notorious band-aids. *Just ask Alice when she's ten feet tall.* As the Red Queen said:

> Nowhere, you see, it takes all the running you can do,
> to keep in the same place. If you want to get some-
> where else, you must run at least twice as fast as that!

How c-c-c-courageous of David to prayerfully declare *"Investigate my life, O God, find out everything about me; Cross-examine and test me, get a clear picture of what I'm about; See for yourself whether I've done anything wrong—then guide me on the road to eternal life."*

It was a week-long retreat setting that did it for me. As individual participants, about twenty in all, we had been taken through a series of therapeutic exercises designed to look within. With all my years of training, education, and background, I could navigate my way through most of the presented models without getting *"touched"* at the deeper core issues of my life. (And yes, we all have issues). Then we did what is called the *"Body Outline."*

If you are not familiar with the term *"Body Outline,"* let me explain. Participants jovially sprawled out on the floor on long pieces of paper. Everyone was excited; humor and giggles filled the air. While some of us lay still, others traced the shapes of our bodies with markers onto the shroud-like wrappings. Afterward, we pinned these alien-shaped figures to the wall and stood eye to eye with images of ourselves.

And there I was. Initially, I laughed at my own odd shape and size. The drawing was not exact, but it was me alright. No getting around it.

Then the moderator gave the instructions: *"Write on your body outline lies that you have been told. Allow the Holy Spirit to prompt you."* These lies, these wounds may have to do with appearance, value, worth—you get the picture. The room was sterile with still-ness. There was no way out. We had to listen within and hear the siren voices we had worked so hard to suppress: mother, father, hus-band, wife, children, siblings, employers, coaches, teachers, friends, enemies, in-laws and out-laws, and even self.

We were to write our false beliefs and distortions that have been driving our lives on a part of the silhouette which correlated with the lies we have embraced. If we were called *"homely,"* we would write it across the face. If we were labeled *"stupid,"* we might scribe it across the head, and so on.

In the safety of true caregivers, everything slowly arose up and out of the depth of our souls. Abusive hurts and emotional scars were scripted in many places too private to note here.

Ashamedly, I wrote my condemning lies in plain sight of all, noting only that everyone was too overwhelmed with their own stuff to bother looking at mine. *"Unworthy." "Good for nothing." "Too fat." "Too lazy." "Why are you even here?"*

The moderator spoke again: ***"What did these lies cost you?"*** I wished she would just shut-up. In obedience, I blazingly scribbled a plethora of consequential losses. Tears were flowing down my cheeks, and not just mine, everyone had been caught. No escape. I felt dangerously vulnerable. My inner toxicity had been exposed. Like a sump pump, pulling all the remaining sludge out of the sickly swamp, I was emotionally spent.

Once these inner wounds were revealed, or at least brought into the light where God could pronounce a new life giving word, I discovered something profound. I no longer feared the inward journey, that long walk down the darkened hallway into solitude and silence. I like myself. God does too. As is. I knew I was *"accepted in the Beloved."*

The accusative stingy voices of my shredded soul were finally squelched. Peace was upon me. Fear disappeared.

Until now, to go within had been much too apprehensive. I had not liked what I heard in the past, so it was a place I had learned to avoid. Like seeing a stranger on a dark night, I quickly crossed to the other side of the street. Don't look, don't stare, don't listen. I covered my ears and made noise, *la, la, la, la, la.*

All along, God was waiting to touch the inward parts. That place where, former disappointments were still remembered despite harried attempts to cloak dreaded yesterdays, where once *all my troubles seemed so far away.* Without God's intervention, they were here to stay.

In most cases, the Christian community focuses its attention on modifying negative behaviors. Rarely are we directed to look at the cause, the core wounds, which may have put us on a path of destructive outcome.

We try to cope with the crises of life the best we can, but our coping mechanisms are usually dysfunctional. They work for a short time; nonetheless, the fallout from the disobliging behavior is as great or greater than the crisis that ignited it. In our search for emotional help, we often simply trade one dysfunction for another.

Instead of trying to address unhelpful and irresponsible conduct, we ought to be sensitively searching for emotionally crippling occurrences that may have deeply affected us long before. We need inner healing.

In our attempts to right the wrongs done to us or by us, we have, with the best of intentions, created more inner chaos. This deepens trauma rather than transforms it. Eventually we realize, to continue in this vein is ludicrous. Like the Prodigal Son, we inevitably must come to our senses and return to the place of origin—*"Our Father in Heaven, Hallowed be Your Name."*

I have been blessed to have been under the tutelage of Dr. Richard Dobbins, the admired Christian Psychologist who started Emerge Ministries in Akron, Ohio. Of his many insightful contributions, there is a poetic formulation that has served me well in ministry and life for many, many years. In a room filled with pastors in training, Dobbins said: ***"Until the pain of remaining the same becomes greater than the pain to change, a person will remain the same."*** Are you there yet?

Our brains have frequently been likened to computers which means we do not forget, especially negatively charged episodes. We try to erase them, maybe even suppress them. Yet, a simple reminder, like a song or a place, stirs up the memory of the event and its destructive effects that we thought were long forgotten.

Applying Scripture to trauma-based catastrophes does help. But it may not heal. We are wired to remember and without direct and specific challenge to those events, we tend to feel and be driven by what our clouded filters are telling us.

Using the Pauline persuasion, *"forgetting those things which are behind,"* as a bandage to what may be bruised and broken is a short-cut to restoration. Forgetting is not what Paul implied, nor what he meant (see appendix). We may mentally press *"delete"* as if effortlessly removing a no longer needed text message, but they are never deleted.

Shhh...Listening For God

Digital images try to convince us by displaying a garbage can with inserted data being hauled off to the dump. Not so. It's all retrievable. Ask retired military man, Ollie North. Delete does not mean delete. Forget does not mean forget. But there is hope.

New episodes that are more pleasant can trump old episodes that were not. Saint Paul presents his case, *"overcome evil with good."* It is a replacement principle.

Ever been afraid to be alone? Me too. I was afraid of myself, my inner voice that always reminded me of my mistakes and faults, shame and blame. It seems before we ever meet God in the silence, we will first meet ourselves. If it was that way for Jesus, we will not escape without inner confrontation either.

> And He was there in the wilderness forty days, tempted by Satan, and was with the wild beasts; and the angels ministered to Him.
>
> Mark 1:13

The inner voice is a powerful accuser. We talk to ourselves all the time, something like 1200-1500 words per minute. That's a constant barrage of 78,000 words an hour, 1,248,000 words a day. Moreover, 70% of them are negative.

I once asked my congregation to wear a rubber band on their wrists from one Sunday to the next. Whenever they had a negative thought about themselves, they were to snap the elastic instrument as a reminder to stop and think differently, to think more scripturally. Capturing every thought to the obedience of Christ takes work I know, but a task when diligently obeyed pays huge dividends (II Cor. 10:4-5).

Many parishioners said they had to quit snapping after just two days as black and blue marks had already appeared on their skin from constant striking.

Silence is much, much more than overcoming negative thinking or turning off the music, the cell phone, and other communitive devices. In the mystic sense, absence of disturbance and/or interruption does not qualify silence as genuine silence. Listening in silence is what makes silence, silence. It is a journey, and like all others, begins with a single step.

Creation began in silence. Many have called the initial moment *"the Big Bang."* My older brother Dennis, student of the stars and physics, reminds me that there was nothing to *"bang." The Big Bang* is a misnomer, a scientific attempt to somehow explain that it all started from a single point of origin. The *"Big Bloom"* would be more like it. *"Nothing in all creation is so like God as silence,"* says Meister Eckhart, Dominican preacher, theologian, and mystic.

Silence is God's first language. The Cosmos is silence in motion. God said, *"Let there be!"* a word issued from Holy Hush. All such words in time and history reflect such power when they come from a period of contemplative stillness. Religious thinker, Gunilla Norris, prompts us:

> Within each of us there is a silence – a silence as vast as the universe. We are afraid of it. . .and we long for it.
>
> When we experience that silence, we remember who we are: creatures of the stars, created from the birth

of galaxies, created from the cooling of this planet, created from the dust and gas, created from the elements, created from time and space. . .created from silence.

Silence is the source of all that exists, the unfathomable stillness where vibration began – the first oscillation, the first word, from which life emerged. Silence is our deepest nature, our home, our own common ground, our peace.

Silence reveals. Silence heals. Silence is where God dwells. We yearn to be there.

Christian thinkers grow concerned about the erosion of silence in our wordy world. Talkativeness runs rampant. *Wordorrhea* is our new disease. I am not the first to write regarding this matter, nor will I be the last.

We are under assault from talk radio, 24/7 news, I-p's like pods and pads, and white noise. We even sleep with sound soothers lest the stillness keep us awake. To lose silence is to drift dangerously into prideful playfulness, whereby we think God's reverential Presence is no longer significant. Noise thus rules the day.

Do you remember the classroom game *"Telephone?"* One student at the front of the class would whisper a statement into the ear of another student. They would whisper what they heard only once into the ear of the next student and so on. This was duplicated until everybody in the room had heard the message.

It was always interesting to know what the last student heard compared to what the first student spoke. This is great illustration of the nature of gossip. However, even more telling is the quietness required to hear a whisper, and to hear it correctly. Due to faulty listening, we could be repeating words, ideas, and notions never intended because they were never spoken in the first place.

Lean into silence. Draw inquisitively close to God, like Isaiah, until we are aware of our inability to say anything worthy of an audience: *"Woe is me, I am one of unclean lips."* Then we hear. We hear the Voice of the Holy, the Almighty, with words so graciously deemed, they penetrate our very spirit. Encountering the living Lord forever changes us, moving us in directions intended by Divine will and loving care.

The very thought that we can be listening for God to speak demands from us a faith perspective. *"For he who comes to God must believe that He is, and that He is a rewarder of them that diligently seek Him."* Science has proven the universe is no accident. Intricate design is defended by the religious and the non-religious. It just is.

In the first statement of the first chapter of the first book of the Bible, there is a Hebrew term (*eth*) basically un-translated. Composed of the first and last letter of the Hebrew alphabet, the *aleph* and a *tau*, it sits in the middle of the most descriptive sentence regarding creation. These two letters appear inconsequential. The possible depiction meaning *"substance or essence"* is considered by some to represent the mind of God, a cosmic conscience, memory, maybe even morality, witnessed in the created order.

In Greek, we would interpret these letters as *alpha* and *omega*. Could this be a reference to Christ in the first verse of Scripture? What's more, the Hebrew letter *tau* written in script is like a capital T—a cross. Could it be *the Lamb slain from the foundation of the world?*

Seth Lloyd, a quantum computer scientist, explores our intricate world in his book, *Programming the Universe*. He cites the double-slit experiment with atomic particles. When observed, particles reacted differently than when unobserved—they somehow knew they were being watched and responded accordingly. Is it weird science or Godness modeled throughout the universe?

British scientists did a study with a plain and simple heat lamp. It was re-wired to randomly turn on or off at varying intervals. All seemed well and good until they placed a box of chirping chicks underneath it. After a short time, the lamp no longer turned on or off haphazardly, but lit up when the chicks chirped for more warmth. No clear scientific answer was supplied as to *"Why."* Researchers declared that the experiment created more questions than it solved.

In the article, *Physics of the Divine*, world renowned Theoretical Physicist, John Polkinghorne, who later became an Anglican Priest, argues his point of belief:

Physics asks how the world works, and when it answers that question it finds a very deep, marvelously patterned order. But it doesn't explain where the order comes from. I believe that the order is a reflection of the mind of God.

The Principle of Nonlocality, a central assumption of Quantum Mechanics, maintains that both things and people are affected by events which are not just in the here and now.

It seems rather apparent that, if we are to discern God's Voice, we must assume God has spoken in the past and continues to speak to us today. The many forms God's Voice may take are beyond imagining. *"Out of the mouths of babes"* should tell us that God's messages are continually coming toward us, yet we are not always aware it is the Lord, fooled by the messenger.

In the realm of God, a jackass can be a suitable medium of expression if need be. Even the crow of a rooster spoke to boastful Peter, reminding him of the former forecast by the Christ now under arrest. Most of all, God uses people of all shapes, sizes, color, and gender. We think of them as ordinary folk, but I prefer to think of them as Angels, Messengers of God. For the *who* is not as significant as the *what*.

When we get right down to the spiritual nitty-gritty, most of the time God is directly speaking to the human heart. Thoughts, dreams, peace, and inner witness, all confirm Divine contact. But the heart is the organ by which we discern, we hear, we listen for the Divine whisper.

God's Voice is softer than most of us perceive. Our Creator did not blare life into existence; God gently breathed it.

From the first whisper long ago, the expansion of the Cosmos continues. God's declarative utterances are full of potential and

Shhh...Listening For God

power. It is necessary that we as God's people partake of the Divine creative ability in each of our lives. One word can go a long way. One word can carry us for a long time.

If we are truly desiring to hear from Heaven, we will need to quiet our personal world. Find a still place or still it yourself. Spiritually pay attention. Ask God to speak. After a time of prayer, linger a bit in expectant anticipation of Divine response. See if you can outlast the many sounds within your own crowded self. Wait. Again, attentively wait some more.

Choice. Let us determine to meet with God. *Decision*. Let us open ourselves to hear from God. *Blessing*. Let us allow ourselves to discern the susurrations of God. *Confirmation*. God speaks in harmony with what has already been creatively spoken. *Remember*. God's spoken Word is always in agreement with God's written Word.

Listening for God Discussion Questions
Chapter 1 – Cosmic Whispers

1. In your own spiritual journey, what are your experiences with the *"upward, inward, outward, forward view of life"* discussed in this chapter?

2. Why does the inward piece take more energy to get started? What is preventing you from starting?

3. Are you always reminded of your mistakes and faults when you become still?

4. Do you agree that silence requires listening?

5. How has God spoken to you? How have these experiences changed your life?

Chapter Two

PICKIN' UP GOOD VIBRATIONS

It was the glittering psychedelic 60s. I had been traveling to New York City for a recording in Capital Studios with a rock band, *The Apple Korps*. On a later visit, our producer, Marty, gave me some free tickets to see the Beach Boys at the famed Carnegie Hall.

At the door, everyone was frisked to make sure no alcoholic beverages or illegal substances entered the great theater. Yeah, right. *"No smoking"* announcements were made continuously, noticeably greeted with jeering boos from the awaiting audience.

The lights went out, the curtain opened, and there was a large flash, as if a thousand people lit matches in a solitary synchronized action. The concert was on. Hallucinogenic vapors filled the air like a thin layer of fog hanging over the highway ahead. We had just crossed over into *"The Twilight Zone."*

By now I was an acknowledged Christian. My life of drugs and alcohol lay strewn on the soiled path behind me. Yup, I inhaled. I sat listening to bouncy tunes with feel-good lyrics—simple, but warm and fuzzy.

Shhh...Listening For God

My attentive gaze was quickly jostled by the offer from a fellow fan seated directly on my right. Somehow he had brought into the event an old gallon, clear glass, vinegar-shaped bottle full of wine. Because my seat was between him and a few of his friends, they offered me *swigs* and *tokes* all evening long. I was the bridge by which all paraphernalia had to cross.

I could deal with the slurred speech and intoxicated moods of those around me. That was not a problem. But my "musical partner" outlandishly and outrageously sang each song. Amazingly, he knew every word to every Beach Boys number, from *"Little Surfer Girl"* to *"Good Vibrations."* He never missed a . . .well, he did miss a few notes, but he never missed a line, except to inhale, hold, swish, and swallow. *O what a night!*

"Good Vibrations" was an international hit for the boys from the sunny West Coast beach. They made it big, but paid a high cost—life, marriages, and more. Fame has its price.

I'm sure you are wondering by now where I am going. So let's segue into the subject of truly *"Good Vibrations."* Karin Bacon rewrote the Beach Boys song to read:

> I'm picking up good vibrations.
> He's giving me excitation.
> I'm picking up good vibrations;
> He's fullness of exultation.
> Good, good, good vibrations.

Jesus is true excitation.
I'm picking up good vibrations.
The Church is true inspiration.

Scientists as well as biologists inform us that all of the created order has vibration. All of God's creatures vibrate. Creation is literally *"dancing energy."*

Discussed by Paul Pearsall, Ph.D., in his book *Making Miracles*, the most important statement Quantum Physics can make about our nature of matter is the description of wave/particle duality. You and I can be equally described as particle or wave, as material or as motion.

Pearsall declares, *"We have life on an energy or 'wave' level in addition to our 'particle' selves."* To view life from the particle side of us is to be bound to the *"it is what it is"* scenario. To view life from the *"energy"* position forever changes how we can live our lives. Everything becomes possibility. New realities are ever expanding for a vibrational universe that's in motion has an integrative tendency about it. We are to participate with the Cosmos and when we do, things called miracles take place more readily. Call it coincidence, call it synchronicity, call it what you like, maybe even Divine providence, God is active.

Long has the scientific community sought to connect the differences between the macroscopic world and the microscopic, knowing in some way they are similar. String theory was the breakthrough, positing that each particle has vibration. Cosmic strings vibrate. Everything is vibration. Everything is frequency. Electrons and protons resonate like tuning forks. Such sensations begin at a cellular level.

New-Agers use the phrase *"Harmonic Convergence"* for a reason. While attending Kent State University in Kent, Ohio, I was introduced to these seemingly bizarre concepts in a philosophy class. There students were taught to *hum* in order to bring our vibes into unity with the vibrations of the Cosmos. As obedient pupils, we would close our eyes in a lotus pose and together we would all join in and *hummmmmm*. Then again, *hummmmmm*. Was this conjoint activity part of a well-rounded education or the more liberal views of a nutty professor?

We never really did converge. Nothing of any big consequence happened. Nobody in the room affirmed new direction or healing of a disturbed conscience. As a matter of fact, life merely continued as it was on the campus and on the globe. Our joint *humming* could not even prevent the deaths of four students in the near months ahead. But there are spiritual implications to all of this.

The law of resonance states, *"Anything that vibrates sympathetically responds to vibrations."* In God's Divine design, creation and creature vibrate and thus can respond to sympathetic vibrations with vibrations. Our very hearing is a result of vibration.

Remember me telling about my severe headaches? Just a bump in the road would jolt my body and send me into levels of agony beyond the numeric scale of 1 to 10. All types of remedies were attempted. Pills, physical therapy, more pills. Things only got worse. God told me, *"I will give you a new song."* I didn't need more music, I thought. *What else do you have?*

Shhh...Listening For God

A pain management physician at the famed Cleveland Clinic finally put two wires up into the back of my skull which are connected to a rechargeable battery in my lower back. I know. I'm wired. These wires vibrate and send a signal to my brain that is interpreted as pleasure instead of pain. Relief at last. Vibration was my cure.

Composer Leonard Bernstein argued, *"Music is at base a set of vibrations called the harmonic series."* Certain created harmonic forms connect with certain emotions, moods, and personalities. The song of the soul affects our health in dramatic ways. We are continually doused with vibrations that consciously or unconsciously set the *"tone and tune"* of our lives.

What about the mysterious Symphony No. 6, *Pathetique*, by Tchaikovsky— a movement creating moods of despair using varying tempos, descending scales and minor keys with several references to death itself. The finale was not the usual noisy *allegro*, but a long drawn-out *adagio*.

Just eight days after sending the work to his publisher, Tchaikovsky was dead, a victim, possibly, of his own depressing tonalilty.

Dr. John Diamond published a book called *Your Body Doesn't Lie*, which investigates the effects of musical vibration on people. With startling results, he noticed, *"The harder the 'rock' the weaker people became."*

Sound has an amazing impact on plants, even water crystals. It seems the beat does make a difference. Guess which plants grow faster and healthier? Those exposed to classical sounds. And so do people. *The Mozart Effect* reveals similar responses. His music can even affect your IQ. On the other hand, plant life actually shuns rock music and leans away from the disruptive noise. Greek Philosopher Aristotle long ago noted:

> Emotions of any kind are produced by melody and rhythm; therefore by music a man becomes accustomed to feeling the right emotions; music has thus the power to form character, and the various kinds of music based on the various moods, may be distinguished by their effect on character. . .

Music is a powerful conveyer of mood, doing things for us and to us. David calmed King Saul's disturbed soul with melodious notes. Worship itself has the same special qualities. Esteemed blind musicologist Fanny Crosby wrote a moving hymn—*"Rescue the Perishing."* Read the words of this stanza, especially the last line:

> Down in the human heart, crushed by the tempter.
> Touched by a loving heart, wakened by kindness.
> Chords that are broken will vibrate once more.

When Scripture and/or Christians speak of unity, we use a musical term, *"harmony,"* to describe the experience. When strife or conflict is present we call it *"disharmony and/or discord,"* which is to say we are not in sync with those around us.

In a perverse sort of way, this *discord* is the *"digital drug"* of the cyber world called *"I-dosing."* By playing opposing musical frequencies (binaural beats) in each ear of a headset a person can reach an altered state, a dangerous high, similar to Ecstasy, Opium, or smoking the wacky weed— *"Mary-Jane."* Out of sync is out of sorts.

According to Novalis, author and philosopher of Early German Romanticism, *"Every disease is a musical problem; every cure is a musical solution."* Dr. Leonard Sweet extends this thought perfectly:

> The discord that jars our culture is a symptom of the greatest disease we currently suffer—the most serious epidemic we now face. The disease is "harmonic clash" – a condition we experience when we find the rhythm of our souls out of harmony with the resonance of God's universe.

Think about it. What makes Jesus our *"great High Priest"* (Hebrews 4:14-15) is His ability to sympathetically vibrate with our circumstantial problems and situational demands. He is touched *[sympatheo]* with the feeling of our infirmities. He has been here, done that, and got the T-shirt kind-of-a-thing. His incarnational life allowed Him to know what it is like to live on this trying planet.

Jesus *sympathizes* with us showing a deep emotional commitment. He feels. People in the world express sympathy with a vocal *ahhhh* to those who have experienced turmoil. But typically it is nothing more than a superficial layer of thin emotion that soon passes or is quickly forgotten.

In contrast, the compassion of the Christ causes Him to take part in our weaknesses and shoulder the infirmities which threaten the health of our human souls. That, my friends, is true *sympatheo*.

Have you ever had the experience of not being able get someone off your mind? No matter what you did, his or her image stayed with you, beckoning a connection of some sort. You might even have started praying or perhaps phone, e-mail or text a word of encouragement that says, IMT *"In my thoughts."*

Usually, the receiving party would acknowledge some kind of quandary and express the joyful gratitude that you cared. Funny, we often respond in such situations with *"Something told me."* Are we afraid to attribute these strange sensations to God? *SomeOne* told me, it is.

Let me ask. Were we following sympathetic vibrations, similar wavelengths, or being led by the Holy Spirit? Could they be one and the same, reflecting a genuine *sonic spirituality* we hardly comprehend?

The vibration of God's Voice has pierced through space and time and matter since its initial proclamation, and continues to move across the Cosmos to this very day. We are born into the Voice of God, says my firstborn son, Joel, physics enthusiast. You and I live within the recurrent frequency of God's creativeness. Our universe is an ongoing vibrating symphony. Every object and every planet has a frequency.

Theoretically, or should I say theologically, humankind has been ever near God's penetrating Presence all along; hearing, feeling, seeing, and detecting wave patterns of Divine Life.

Uniquely, each human body has its own distinct frequency or wave length. Some may call this the human aura or the electromagnetic field that represents every individual.

Despite the cinema-graphic images of Hollywood's sci-fi dazzling visual effects, we must accept the reality that humans cannot pass through other objects and/or matter. We do not anatomically match the frequency or the wave pattern of the object we are trying to get through and so we are repelled like two magnets with the same polarity resisting each other.

We have seen many a Superhero leap over a tall building in a single bound, and with splintering debris, crash through a building with brute force. Jesus, however, in a resurrected state, exhibited a fascinating ability to pass through the walls of the Upper Room without destructive disturbance, eat a meal, and exit without ever opening a door or window. Won't eternity be fun?

So how much strength do we possess as electromagnetic individuals enveloped by the Spirit of the living God? An eccentric inventor, Nikola Tesla, envisioned that a single individual could knock down any tall building with the matching power of sympathetic vibration—a gentle nudge at the right time.

Have you ever pushed a child on a swing? After each extended arch, the child returns to the position of starting and we gently push again matching the sympathetic cycle of the swing. As we repeatedly push, the child swings further and higher responding to the synchronized motion.

Tesla discovered that everything is vibrating. Everything. If we could sympathetically add energy to each vibration, we could accentuate the vibration to be greater and stronger each time. According to

Shhh...Listening For God

Tesla, one person could topple the Empire State Building by gently synchronizing a sequence of thrusts to the natural sway or vibration of the structure. Just like the child on the swing, eventually it would sway further and further until *"tilt!"*

Many buildings globally are now constructed to withstand the quaking and shaking of our planet. But no building can withstand the gentle synchrony of sympathetic vibrations, technically called mechanical resonances. Things we consider sturdy can wobble like a top out of control and come crashing down. Tesla has proven it. And *MYTHBUSTERS* dabbled with his theories.

How about the seemingly overly dramatic battle of Jericho? Having walked the ancient site several times, I have witnessed up close the massive thick walls just as the Bible describes them. How could the wandering Israelites overcome such a stronghold by simply marching around the enormous battlements and tooting their horns at specific times? Perhaps sympathetic vibration played a role.

Archeologists state that the walls of this once great city fell outward which is strange in itself. If a fortress was being attacked, typically the walls would collapse inward, pushed by the advancing movement of the attackers. Not so here.

It would be worth your while to Google Tesla's experiments and read more about this *Mad Scientist,* as his neighbors used to call him. In 1898 he experimented with an electromechanical oscillator no bigger than a small analog alarm clock. After attaching it to an iron pillar in his apartment, he patiently waited for the resonance

Shhh...Listening For God

of each to match. He nearly collapsed the building he lived in and rattled several others nearby.

On another occasion, by clamping a vibrating oscillator to one of the beams, Tesla violently shook the iron framework of a ten story building in the Wall Street district of New York. Sympathetic vibration is an amazingly powerful reality.

What if we, the Christian Church, could walk together in unity? Military participants are aware of this resounding truth. Marching in formational stride, troops are ordered out of step when crossing a bridge lest the resonance of the march match the resonance of the bridge and collapse that which is to carry them across to the other side.

I have even read that certain tones sung in unison could crack the supporting pillars of any stadium if the resonance of the song matched the resonance of the structure. What would happen if congregations embraced the concept of unity in their worship? Could we topple the kingdom of darkness and break its grip upon the human race? Sympathetically, I think so. *Let the Saints go marching in!*

Vibrational resonance begins very early in the Bible. I have a belief that if we could understand the first couple of chapters of the book of Genesis we could better understand the rest of Holy Writ. We may even better understand how life was created and how we are to function in this ordered system of ours.

"And God said. . ." This may seem a bit terse, a mere three word phrase. But it portrays the Creator in a speaking posture from the very outset. Reformer, Martin Luther, stated, "God is a *deus*

Shhh...Listening For God

loguens—a speaking God." The psalmist proclaims, *"The voice of the LORD is powerful; the voice of the LORD is full of majesty."*

The stance of our Creator is as speaker. The stance of creation and creature is listener. When Inspired Text is particularly investigated, a listening posture is the focus; a position not of straining to see, or stressing to say, but situated to hear.

Life is more than vision. Life is more than confession. It is vibration. Listen up. Receive from it. Connect with it.

The evening news in my area, Cleveland, Ohio, announced that 66% of people hear phantom cellular tones and vibrations which do not exist. How many times have I picked up my own cell phone thinking it had quivered. I'm positive it vibrated in my pocket, I could feel it. Rapidly, I look for activity only to discover the same old screen saver with no new calls displayed. Discernment of what surrounds us could be one of the most important developments of the cyber era.

Cosmic vibrations are arriving at the entrances of our souls at an alarming rate of repetition every day. Intentionality thus becomes a most important term.

As followers of Christ, we must be intentional about positioning ourselves for *"God Vibrations."* We will need to place ourselves in prayerful listening to both His directive Voice and commanding Word. We must come to terms with the necessity of setting aside some quiet time to be with God. Silence is important. If not, as Henri

Shhh...Listening For God

Nouwen has penned, *"We do not take the spiritual life seriously."* I do. I know you do as well.

Living in a football town, metaphors abound from the sport that makes people do crazy things. Here in Cleveland, the *"Dawg Pound"* is notorious; it's that one section on the end of the field where true fans are exceptionally fanatical. It is not uncommon to see dog ears, dog noses, and dog faces as signs of support. At one time, the opposing team would be pelted with dog bones if they neared the goal line.

In Cleveland, we love our defense probably because we haven't seen much offense for a long time. During a game, the announcers will undoubtedly utter this observant comment— *"The defense is getting tired."* Being on the field play after play without adequate rest takes its toll as the game approaches the final quarter.

In the many years that I have cheered the brown and orange, never have I heard a sportscaster declare— *"The offense is getting tired."* Never. Offense feeds the frenzy of scoring points and winning games.

As Christians who live in hostile territory, it's time we go on the offense. Too long we have hidden behind our shields of faith trying to deflect *"all the fiery darts of the wicked one."* Why not mount up with wings as eagles? Why not take the sword of the Spirit and forcibly advance? Why not cast down temptations before they become strongholds?

Tend to your offense! Take authority! Control the varied vibrations that are going on in your life. Offense keeps the Devil backing up. Offense keeps you moving forward. On offense you are able to excessively celebrate victories in the end zone of life without penalty. Then you will truly enjoy *"Good Vibrations."*

Ready? Let's go!

Listening for God Discussion Questions
Chapter 2 – Pickin' Up Good Vibrations

1. Do you believe we are created to respond to vibrations?

2. How does music impact your life?

3. How does your life change when viewed from the *"wave/energy"* position?

4. When have there been times when you experienced a *"deep emotional commitment"* with another person or situation? Why do you think that happened?

5. As divinely created vibrational beings, how are we to negotiate the world around us?

6. How do you feel about the Cleveland Browns?

Chapter Three

HALLOWED BE THY TIME

When the decision was made to build a new worship facility to sustain our growing church membership, certain tasks needed to be addressed. A location needed to be determined, monies needed to be raised, and an architect needed to be found.

After the first two matters were accomplished, we started interviewing several skilled innovators in the field of design. The process was time consuming, but we finally selected our man. Next, we needed to prepare structural drawings of the building, which could not happen without getting to know the spatial requirements of the congregation.

One evening, the architect asked me why he was chosen over the many who had applied for the task at hand. Without hesitation, I immediately responded to him. In our initial discussion phase, he expressed an understanding of several important factors that up until now were unique to my own limited theology.

We chose him because this artist of the Eternal Kingdom was rightly concerned about certain specific design areas: people flow for saintly fellowship (*God is love*), illumination for appropriate theatrical productions (***God is light***), and audio-visual/multi-media applications (***God is sound***). This trinitarian awareness is precisely what we needed.

Most likely we are familiar with the scriptural descriptions—*God is love*, *God is light*. Have we missed the nuance of a speaking God, that *God is sound* as well?

In the creation event, God filled the darkened void, speaking into it with Holy utterance. All matter listened and responded to Spirit Voice, taking on the form and function Divinely intended. God created the Cosmos with a breath.

The mathematical precision of the Cosmos indicates a mathematician as its Designer. Both the universe and the Bible demonstrate theomatic overlaps, the recurrent theme of numeric preciseness. The Cosmos is not an accident, but a delicate orchestration of events. In a sense, the universe is one big piece of music. In the fascinating book *Sacred Geometry*, Stephen Skinner cites:

> If you draw the bow of a violin over a tuned metal plate sprinkled with light powder. . .the grains line up in complex patterns. So not only do sacred numbers govern planetary orbits and musical harmony, but those notes also create beautiful geometrical forms.

Jewish theologian Abraham Heschel stated, *"First we sing. Then we believe."* In essence, music made us before we ever made music. Music is part and parcel of our DNA, which carries the plans of constructing unique you*ness*.

Shhh...Listening For God

If all the DNA molecules of an individual were compacted, they would fit in the space of an ice cube. If stretched out end to end, that same DNA would extend from the earth to the moon nearly 8,000 times.

According to the molecular biologists, the DNA of each individual has his or her own individual melody. By placing the DNA strand that defines us on its side, like the keyboard of a piano, we discover that God has written a special song directly on the human soul.

Physicists declare that the electron shell of the carbon atom follows the laws of harmonics. It produces a musical scale of C, D, E, F, G, A. These very notes form the hexachord of the Gregorian Chant. Could it be that all carbon-based life is built on these ancient tones?

With all the countless forms music has taken throughout the centuries, it is the calming, pleasing gradation of the Gregorian Chants that speaks to the human soul regarding its spiritual existence. No matter who we are or what our stylistic preferences, the ethereal qualities of the melodic symmetry connect us to what is called the Divine. Who would have thought that a group of chanting monks would be leading global revitalization, a movement within?

Gregorian Chants consist of a single melody sung either by a soloist, choir, or responsively between them. There are no instruments. It is widely believed that they were derived from Jewish Chant since their earliest forms can be traced back to ancient Israel.

It was in the Middle Ages that Gregorian Chants assumed the traditional form known today. Around the world these cantillations are sung everyday in the public service of praise and worship throughout the canonical hours, especially by monastic choirs.

The Chants, seemingly in *"timeless fascination,"* speak to the human heart with a universal call to stop and enter the now, to heed the message of the moment. Ever so graciously, they speak to the monk in all of us which longs to connect to the ultimate source of meaning and value. David Steindl-Rast and Sharon Lebell note in their *Music of Silence, A Sacred Journey Through the Hours of the Day:*

> Saturated with information but often bereft of meaning, we feel caught in a never-ending swirl of duties and demands, things to finish, things to put right. Yet as we dart anxiously from one activity to the next, we sense that there is more to life than our worldly agendas.

We have distorted time. For westerners, time is always running out. Time is thought of as a limited commodity. Thus, we end up making countless contributions to its march: *Hurry up! Come on! We're gonna be late!*

Gregorian Chants evoke a different relationship to time. In the Chants, time flows harmoniously *"in proportion to the task at hand."* Gregorian Chants remind us of other possible ways to live, they invite our souls to choose a more solemn path, to stop talking and start listening.

Thomas Mann, late German author and Nobel laureate, believed that music was the gauge of a healthy civilization. How vibrational tones affect the various dimensions of our beings is just starting to be seriously explored. But music therapy has always been a practitioner's scalpel. If a bit melancholy, better watch what we listen to or we might find ourselves involved in a blues riff taking us down the slippery slope toward *"gloom, despair, and agony on me."*

Japanese research scientist, Susumu Ohno, translated the musical notes of a funeral march by Chopin into chemical equations. The composition of the music was almost identical to a cancer gene found in humans. Makes one wonder what negative vibrations may be penetrating our seemingly ungarrisoned inner lives.

The word from which we get *"to sing"* (cantare) means to *"work magic"* and/or *"to heal."* In ancient times, a Cantor was someone who healed with sounds and music. A Cantata, thus, was a healing piece of music. Hebrews sang psalms to heal the sick and the Talmud offered selected songs that could protect the physical body from infirmity. Music not only creates us, it is what keeps us going.

"Take heed what you hear" said Jesus. Each of us must take responsibility for what is coming our way in the form of vibrational influence. After my conversion, having been a former long haired rock n' roller, it became necessary for me to critically filter what came in and out of my being. Sound can be damaging.

In my middle ages, I scheduled myself for a hearing test. I sat in a soundproof room with padded earmuffs as the attendant beeped high and low frequencies into my claustrophobic mindless accommodation. With eyes closed, I would intensely try to discern the mosquito-like sounds as if I were going to win a valuable prize.

Shhh...Listening For God

When the exam was finally finished, I stepped out into the main office. The attendant's first words were, *"Played rock music did ya?"* The loss of significant tones in the appropriate ranges was that apparent.

Sound comes at us daily and from differing spheres. Some good, some bad, some healthy, some evil, some death laden with interference. As members of the 21st century, we are bombarded with auditory signals. Greeting cards now have sound chips blaring a message to the unsuspecting opener.

Noise is seemingly everywhere, rarely are we without it. Have you ever been threatened by booming voices from above? Attention MALL shoppers! *"Even if the Word of God was proclaimed, it would not be heard or heeded because there's too much noise and busyness in our world,"* said Kierkegaard.

Richard Foster, in his classic *Celebration of Discipline*, captures effectively the celestial conflict. ***"In contemporary society our Adversary majors in three things: noise, hurry, and crowds."***

Purchased a vehicle in the last decade or so? A computed voice from somewhere unknown tells us everything, a seemingly galactic star from another realm. Directions. Warnings. Exhortations. *Change the oil! Door ajar! Seat belt! Turn here!* We can even pick the gender and nationality of our embedded guide, if so desired. But we will have noticeable difficulty removing these auricular intrusions.

Our noisy society has gone as far as to attempt the trademark of certain recognizable sounds. The NBC chimes. The roaring lion of

MGM. The distinct *vroom* of a Harley-Davidson motorcycle. If only we could trademark God's Voice.

My book began with a safe assumption. God speaks. Characteristics of voice and sight, hearing and response, set the One and true apart from *"dumb idols"* which do not involve themselves in the human drama. God is speaking. Moreover God desires dialogue. We need to hear and respond. Why don't we?

As a pastor, I recurrently pray with people in need of God's leading light. Many are seeking healing from dire afflictions and directions from dire circumstances. *"Life comes at you fast."* Most frequently the culprit is *dis-ease*; the infirmed are out-of-harmony with God, life, others, and quite often themselves.

A concert piano has 240 strings and when tuned and tightened, the tension equals 40,000 pounds of pull on the frame. Without that tension, there would be no musical sound from its ebony and ivory keys of black and white. But if there is too much tension, the frame will not contain the pull and will begin to crack under the strain, thus destroying the music and the very instrument designed to express it.

Over-commitments alone can knock us out of tune and rob us of life's serenades. Just how many charming compositions have we failed to hear, all at the cost of hurriedness? Songwriter and recording artist Jamie Smith takes the invitation of Jesus and presents it to us in poetic rhythm:

Why do you linger? Why do you wait? You carry on without Me. I've always been there, still you hesitate. I have much in store for you if only you would. . .Come unto Me, all you who are weary. Come unto Me, all you who need rest. Take up my yoke and learn all about Me and I will give you rest. Sweet rest.

Workaholism is one of the acceptable addictions according to worldly standards, an apprised ethic. However, Eugene Peterson pulls back the curtain exposing this cosmetic wizardry. *"Busy is a symptom, not of commitment but of betrayal."*

Violation of the spiritual discipline of Sabbath can cost us. Look at Israel. They paid dearly in the Old Testament for ignoring God's command and example of sequential rest. Even the Land was to experience Sabbath every seventh year, thus fostering future quality and quantity.

When working late all the time, I unintentionally invite certain stress related issues into my body, and in this way, *somatize* my stress. Headaches, body aches, and emotional aches can be attributed to work without boundaries. We cannot continually and repeatedly violate the rules of Sabbath and get away with it. God takes the Day of Rest rather seriously. It is the first feature of creation called holy.

History records that France at one time cancelled the Sabbath model in an act of religious persecution. Such obligations were considered elements of mere mysticism. The health of the inhabitants was so ill-affected that the Sabbath was restored, not for spiritual reasons, but for physical and mental betterment.

God initiated a rest most early in the biblical passages of creation (Genesis 2:2). I'm sure it was not exhaustion from a long week at the office. Conversely, God introduced a powerful paradigm for

Shhh...Listening For God

wellness. The climax of the seventh day was not the creating of creature, but the creating of tranquility, that one thing the universe still lacked.

Dr. Gerald Schroeder, physicist and theologian, says God did not rest on the Sabbath. *"Rather the Creator caused a repose to encompass the universe that had been made during the first six days."*

Meet *El Olam*; the Everlasting God, the God of the Ages who works in stages. Creation was not done in one day but six. God is in no hurry. God will keep Covenant and Promise no matter how long it takes, just ask Abraham or Joseph.

Believe it or not, you and I have all the time in the world. For humans, time is not linear or directional, but circulatory, spontaneous, coincidental, interwoven, even suddenly surprising.

Christians should understand more than anyone else, that time is timeless, that past, present, and future are not separate. They are connected said the prophets and priests and now say the physicists. We can slow down. We can be patient. As the songwriter, Chris Tomlin says:

> Age to Age He Stands,
> And time is in His Hands;
> The Beginning and the End,
> The Beginning and the End;
>
> How great is our God!
> Sing with me...
> How great is our God!
> And all will see how great,
> How great is our God!

Shhh...Listening For God

In retrospect, Adam and Eve were given a Sabbath after doing no work, at least nothing that would require a day off. Humankind must surrender its locus as the pinnacle of the creation account. Sabbath was and is special time, set apart for hallowed treatment. Apparently, quiet and rest, silence and solitude are valuable parts of the rhythms of life and must be respected.

In the beginning chapters of Genesis, God is pictured as the One who does all the work. God blesses from an abundance of grace. God provides a garden and more. Concernedly, God shows Adam where all the gold is. The Lord gives Adam and eventually Eve everything they need. They pray no prayer. They claim no promise. But they do trustingly rest in the provision of the Covenant Keeper.

Why a Sabbath? Some have said it exists simply so that we do not make our lives too hectic, as if everything that is going well is from our own personal hard work and dedication. The Deuteronomist warns: *"Beware lest you forget it is the LORD who has blessed you, otherwise you may say in your heart, my power and the strength of my hand has made me this wealth."*

While in Jerusalem, I attended Synagogue on the eve of what they call *Shabbat*. Near the end of the service, the devout turned around and faced the entrance and welcomed in the Sabbath as a bride. Like a gathering of family and friends which rises on a special note from the organist, *"Here comes the bride veiled in white,"* we stood in expectant anticipation. This simple incident changed my perspective forever.

Shhh...Listening For God

What would happen if we approached time more matrimoniously? Would we treat her with more tenderness, more reverence? Would we care for her more delicately? Certainly we would respect her value with awe and dignity.

The Sabbath and its holiness are the Lord's way of getting us alone, getting us quiet enough to hear. In a society that worships work, works at play, and plays at worship, the Day of Rest is the wisdom of God—at work. It holds a significant role in positioning us to listen.

Teresa of Avila said, *"Settle yourself in solitude and you will come upon Him in yourself."* The Sabbath provides such a practice. As for me, I take many mini Sabbaths all day long, all week long. These special moments, breaks in routine, quench the clamoring sounds of *"tinkling cymbals."*

What is twisted is our Sabbath substitutions. We are disconnected at many levels. Look at us, we purchase CDs of nature. Check out the stores. Offered are recordings of rain, chirping birds, waves on the beach, storm, and waterfalls. Do you mean to tell me we believe that this is acceptable diversion? Again, space and opportunity are filled with pseudo auditory signals as a background to help us stay focused on current deadlines of productivity. How sad. Speed is the god of the current culture.

Attending a pastoral conference, I found myself sitting on hard chairs for two full days of lectures. My brain was full *("May I be excused?")* and my body was starting to groan. Experiencing a *"pain*

Shhh...Listening For God

in the neck" which severely radiated to my shoulder, I thought I'd better go outside to stretch.

Lying on the grass, I looked up leisurely and scanned the wild blue yonder. Cloud watching was a thing of the past, something of childhood fantasy. At the moment, it was an attempt at relaxation, a Sabbath break.

I began talking to God. After a few moments, I turned on my side, but found no relief. I turned to the other side trying to stop the escalating pain, 10 + on the radiating grimace scale. Just then, a fluttering white butterfly unhesitatingly approached and landed on my cheek. It ever so lightly freckled my face for 20 seconds and flew away. I knew I had been kissed.

Such tenderness was better than the laying on of hands or the working of miracles. God had spoken again. And I heard the Voice, for I was correctly postured and spiritually positioned to hear with the heart. God loves me. God is with me. Always.

In Jerusalem, I have friends, Darla and Oz, who live directly across from the Old City. From their living room, we can sit and stare at the Upper Room and Temple Mount in awe. We revel in history right before our very eyes.

Whenever I visit the Holy City, I am afforded lodging with this loving couple, a relationship from childhood days. We rehearse our memories, gingerly stroll through Zion Gate, and head down to the Western Wall for prayer.

But on Friday, prior to the beginning of Sabbath, there is a flurry of activity. Before the stores close and the taxis stop running, special foods are purchased and everything is prepared in advance. Sabbath is celebratory.

It would be good for all of us to experience at least one Israeli Sabbath. It is quite amazing that the entire Nation stops to honor and remember the command of their God. On this day, literally we do nothing. We sleep, talk, eat, nap, rejoice, and rest, but no work. And it all begins by attending Synagogue and with a prayer by the Rabbi.

In this fast-lane age, resting on the Sabbath is extremely difficult for everyone. Malls, banks, and businesses are now open seven days a week. Work schedules demand day after day of endless corporate dedication or lose employment to the long list of eager job pursuers.

Sunday has become the one day in which to crunch shopping, family, fellowship, sports, and a host of other pressing demands. Church attendance gets in the way and is sadly the easiest piece for some to extract from their crowded lives.

Once upon a time, people determined their calendar and day through the movement of the Cosmos; literally, *Solar Time*. But Israel was called by God to live on *Sacred Time*, to be governed by Divine manifestation in lieu of circling contraptions. Passover, the seventh month on the solar calendar, was moved to be the first month of calculations for the Jewish year. Redemptive events determined the unfolding story of time.

Shouldn't we also, as people of redemption, resist the frantic pace of daily demands which overwhelmingly determines our schedule? Our alleged time-saving geek gadgets jingle a recognizable sound that says we really are at the whim of the clock. **God desires that miraculous moments episodically mark our memory of** *sacred time* **with demonstrations of spiritual power and Holy Ghost intervention.**

Without special recognition of time's sacred value, much may be frittered away in wasteful practices. Waiting and quietness may appear on the surface to be of little merit, useless when we could be *"doing"* other things. Max Lucado in his *Applause of Heaven* notes his own perspective:

> When I was 10 years old, my mother enrolled me in piano lessons. . .Spending thirty minutes every afternoon tethered to a piano bench was torture. . .Some of the music though, I learned to enjoy. I hammered the staccatos. I belabored the crescendos. . .But there was one instruction in the music I could never obey to my teacher's satisfaction. The rest. The zigzagged command to do nothing. What sense does that make? Why sit at the piano when you can pound? "Because," my teacher patiently explained, "music is always sweeter after a rest."

Pure time spent with God has no equal. It is of untold equity, an earthly deposit reaping eternal dividends. Honor the Sabbath. In the act of slowing down we may just hear wisdom speak, dispensing her guidance. Wisdom comes with two hands says Solomon: *"Length of days is in her right hand. In her left hand riches and honour"* (Proverbs 3:16).

Shhh...Listening For God

Be at peace. Waste some time with God. Implement the practice of Sabbath. Let us hallow our days on earth. Amen.

Shhh...Listening For God

Listening for God Discussion Questions
Chapter 3 – Hallowed Be Thy Name

1. Do you think that all people long to connect to the *"ultimate source of meaning and value?"*

2. How do you practice Sabbath?

3. What does Sabbath mean to you?

4. Have you had an experience something like the *"kiss of a butterfly?"*

5. When do you *"waste time"* with God?

Chapter Four

HEAR YE, HEAR YE, HEAR YE

My parents used to say to me, *"God gave you two ears and one mouth for a reason."* And??? We are supposed to listen twice as much as we talk; now a forgotten bit of wisdom but so, so true.

It has been said, that as humans approach death, hearing is the final sense of experience. Whereas spiritually, when the ways of Divine Life are abandoned, it seems hearing is the first of our senses to depart. Thus, we find solitude and silence uncomfortable, although they are the very disciplines needed to discern Heavenly messages which differ from our own.

It is no coincidence that the central prayer of Jewish life is, *"Hear, O Israel: the LORD our God, the LORD is one!"* Out of 5,845 verses they could have chosen to implement into their daily routines, it is the term *"Hear"* which is so fervently esteemed.

This passage, Deuteronomy 6:4, is so revered it is the first section of Scripture that a Jewish child learns. Called the *Shema* (titled after the first word *"Hear"* in Hebrew), it is recited three times daily, once in the morning (to set their minds on God), once at midday (to serve as a reminder), and once in the evening (to ward off the dangers of the night). Each day is to start and end with hearing.

On the right doorpost of every Jewish home or business is a *Mezuzah*, a decorative cylinder containing select papered passages of honored texts. Upon entering, the resident, guest or patron will kiss his or her fingers and touch the esteemed object with remembrance of its scripted contents. This act of dedication is reverently practiced so that the Scripture will be truly heard and written upon the heart.

On the front of the *Mezuzah* is sometimes an engraved Hebrew symbol that looks like a modern free-hand capital (שׁ). This Hebraic letter, the *Shin,* provides the *"Sh"* for words like *Shalom* or *Shema.* However, on the mounted enclosure, the *Shin* is an abbreviated reminder of *El Shaddai,* the One who pours forth blessings into empty vessels.

If you have ever seen an episode from the original TV series *"Star Trek,"* then you were introduced to Spock, a pointy eared alien character. He was a Vulcan with unique abilities. His distinct planetary salute was a separated trilogy of fingers held uprightly, a feat imitated only by the coordinated, not one of my virtues. His 3-pointed gesture reflects the *Shin,* in Hebrew thought—God.

Amazingly, the Name of God is topographically displayed by the Hebrew letter *Shin.* It is inscribed into the landscape by the three valleys of Jerusalem (which can be seen by satellite) that mark the city as God's. For some, the *Shin* denotes Jerusalem as the central point of the whole earth.

Beginning from the west to the east, the three valleys would be the *Gehenna,* the *Tyropoeon* (which forms the southward slope of the Western Wall), and the *Kidron.* These three descents converge below the City of David and fulfill future prophecy as water from the Temple area will eventually proceed *"down"* to the Dead Sea bringing new life to an undrinkable salty lake rich with minerals.

From *Shalom* to *Shaddai* to *Shema,* the *Shin* signifies these special terms of endearment. Thus, much can be said regarding the monotheistic declaration of the *Shemaic* text, *"Hear O Israel. . ."* sure enough. And as God commanded, it is important to understand all that the passage is communicating. But all is for naught if one is not inclined to *"Hear."* That is the point.

To assist with the hearing of the passage, Orthodox Jews pronounce each word very carefully. To eliminate distraction, they cover their eyes with the palm of their right hand. Since the *Shema* reaffirms the basic tenets of Jewish faith, it is important to hear clearly and distinctly what they are saying, and what God is saying in the process.

Jesus acknowledged the significance of the *Shema:* **"The first of all the commandments is: 'Hear, O Israel: the LORD our God, the LORD is one.'"** Reciting the Deuteronomic context is called *"The acceptance of the yoke of the kingship of God."* For those who do hear, *"How blessed are your ears."* Apparently not everyone who listens, hears.

At the time Jesus lived, devout Jews wore scriptural texts in little boxes called phylacteries on their foreheads. This was done in compliance with God's command *"And thou shalt bind them for a sign upon thine hand, and they shall be as frontlets between thine eyes"* (Deuteronomy 6:8). The *Shema*, of course, was included in the compartment.

One of the clashes Jesus had with the religious of His time was that they *"made broad their phylacteries"* (Matthew 23:5). The Scripture boxes were attached with ribbons wrapped around the left forearm and around the forehead, tied in a knot at the back of the neck. It quickly became a spectacle that had lost its original meaning.

The Christian *"Sign of the Cross"* widely used in the early church was called a *"transfiguration of Jewish devotional life."* The external act of marking oneself with a Cross was similar to *phylacteria*, to guard and protect oneself, as well as to remind the bearer who he or she was and whom they represented.

While Testamental symbols serve as valid witnessing, too often their significance has been forgotten. In that case we find ourselves going through the motions, mere obligatory tokenism. The spiritual pattern started with *"Hear, O Israel."* Are we still listening? Remember the emphasis *"Hear"*. . .not *"See, O Israel,"* or *"Speak, O Israel,"* but *"Hear ye, Hear ye, Hear ye!"*

Some years ago, I briefly toured Italy. Rome is a must see. And yes, when in Rome do as the Romans do—visit the Sistine Chapel. Breathtaking, too marvelous to describe. The artistic quality is beyond comprehension, while at the same time colorfully reflecting the theological content we are addressing. One small point in the whole scope of the hushed interior is the portrayal of the biblical characters.

How does Michaelangelo differentiate between the Major and Minor Prophets? The Major Prophets are listening, not prophesying. Isaiah says *"Incline your ear, and come unto Me. Hear, and your soul shall live."*

I remember reading a story about a lady, a peering passenger in a small prop plane, Janice Gravely. While in flight to Statesboro, Georgia, her husband Edmund died at the controls. Although inexperienced, she managed to keep the craft aloft for nearly two hours.

Janice said she prayed. . .sang hymns. . .prayed. . .sang. . .prayed. She kept radioing for support through the entire ordeal—*"Help! Help! Can't someone help me. . . my pilot is unconscious!"*

Eventually the plane ran out of fuel and crashed. She crawled for hours and made her way to a farmhouse where she received the necessary medical assistance. Authorities said, *"We got the distress signal, but before we could respond, she would switch channels."*

I wonder if we are like Janice? We need God. Desperately we want Divine help, but we never seem to be on the same channel. *Belief. Doubt. Belief. Doubt, doubt, faith, faith, maybe. . .*

Every once in awhile I use a transistor radio to listen to a Cleveland sporting adventure. The dial is not digital. It moves a bar through a sequence of numeric station identifiers. No jumping to the next designated digit, I must glide my way through the static until I get the proper reception. Then the monophonic hubbub pops in loud and clear. Like fine tuning an instrument, I proceed a little past the true note, or a little under and make my way to pitch.

Hearing God is very much like hearing that old radio signal. God's Voice is out there, beaming in clear and strong, however, spiritual static often prevents our receiving the message. Ever ask on what frequency is God? AM is different from FM. Digital is different from analog. Spiritual is different from sensual. Silence is different from sound.

In cell-phonic jargon, it is the number of bars displayed which tells you of your receptivity. The more vertical lines, the fewer dropped calls. Perhaps more time listening equates to more bars and signals greater openness to God.

It was the early 70s, I had just graduated from college and was working in downtown Cleveland as a photographer in the silk screen processing business. We made large and small signs for taxi cabs, buses, billboards, and more. I enjoyed my graphic arts position, but the drive to and from work was grinding. Experiencing wind effect snow off the Great Lake, Erie, made winter travel treacherous. Leaving early and arriving home late made for times when I never saw daylight throughout the gray, gloomy Cleveland winter months.

I never understood why they call traffic snarls *"Rush Hour."* Rarely could we get to work from the suburbs to the inner city in sixty minutes. And never was there a rush. It was a nail biting, dash pounding, teeth clenching, and tightly gripped steering wheel of a

Shhh...Listening For God

ride (sounds like an amusement park). Bumper to bumper, one horn to another, slowly we crept into the city, only to repeat the entire ordeal eight hours later.

Coming home was always an emotionally conflicting commute. The joy of leaving polluting exhaust and rabid road rage brought an anticipated sensation of relief. Nonetheless, the tension pent-up in the process took much longer to release than the ride itself, sometimes even hours. I learned through hard knocks not to do anything too demanding when I finally arrived home. Unwind, greet the kids, say a prayer, get a bite to eat. That was it.

I was a relatively new Christian and enjoying the worshipfulness of Holy Presence. My heart was overflowing with love for Jesus and a deep desire to be led by His Spirit. Reading the book of Acts made me realize miracles are still for us today.

It was a typical work day. . .long, hard, and tiresome. The drive home was similar to all others, filled with stress and anxiety. As I came through the back door of my three bedroom, one bath bungalow, I heard within my heart the word of the Lord quite clearly— *"Call Don. Now."*

Don was the lead vocalist, guitarist, and pianist in our local band. He was a brilliant individual in every way. High IQ, a genius at everything. Give him space and a book or an instrument and he would have it mastered in a short time.

"Call Don. Now." This time the Voice of the Lord seemed a little more forceful. My response was *"Sure, I'll call. Just let me settle*

Shhh...Listening For God

in for a bit. Please Lord, allow me to de-frag, greet my children, kiss my wife, pet the dogs. I'll call right after supper." "Call Don. Now!" came once again, a little louder, more firmly and directly.

I decided this was a test of inner obedience. If I were going to learn God's Voice, I had better practice, practice, practice. I asked my family for a break to make a quick call. Really I had nothing to say and no real reason for calling except to get God off my back. I found a quiet spot in the house and dialed.

Don quickly answered—*"Hello." "Hi,"* I said. *"It's Neal."* The other end was quiet. So I chimed in steering the conversation. *"I felt the Lord wanted me to call you and tell you everything is going to be alright."* Don simply whispered a soft response, *"Okay,"* and hung up.

Don's brilliance made him a little eccentric. A great guy who would do anything for anyone. A young Christian himself, nonetheless, his artistic personality took him on emotional rides from bottom to top and back again.

Unknown to me, Don had just been dumped by a girl he dearly loved. As Christians, Don and I no longer cried in our beers, but we had not yet gained the insight on how to prayerfully process emotional hurt and harm.

At the moment of my pole-to-pole, wired connection, Don was clutching a weapon and was contemplating the worst of the worst. But before pulling the trigger of the gun aimed at his head, he uttered a simple prayer to Jesus. *"If you are real, give me a sign."* That's not a prayer I recommend anyone praying, for it is conditioned on a lot of *"dotted "i's and crossed t's."*

The phone ringing in the air was Don's sign that God was real and cared. Don is still with us writing songs, playing instruments, getting along in life. I am humbled to have been used at such a crucial juncture.

What if I had not heard God's Voice? What if I had not surrendered in obedience and responded to God's request? I shudder to think of the outcome. It was a dramatic learning curve for me. God speaks.

Hearing from God is not as difficult as it sounds. I admit, however, that we have to somehow distinguish the Divine Voice from the many that come our way in a given day.

Ever have good friends call on the phone? Assuredly, they never introduce themselves with some formal expression of name, rank, and serial number. They safely assume that we recognize their voices. How can they do that? The answer is repetitional interaction. Over time, we learn the voices of our friends and they learn ours. Every voice is quite distinct in pitch, tone, inflection, and accent. The true listener becomes a master of detection, even when certain people try to disguise themselves in a humorous attempt at surprise.

Learning God's Voice happens in a similar way. Once we discern God speaking, it becomes easier and easier to hear. Once in awhile, doubt may enter and we must unclutter our souls from distractions which block any clear understanding of Divine interchange.

For me, listening for God all started years ago with desire. I wanted to hear from God's Spirit. I sought Divine direction. I prayed

Shhh...Listening For God

for God's guiding Hand to steer my life in a most supernatural way. My prayers, lifted up with simple longing, have all been answered. You can pray similar prayers and receive similar responses.

Sometimes I just ask, *"God, is this You? If so, keep speaking and confirm Your Voice to me."* I search my soul for an inner witness. I search Scripture for an outward confirmation. Then I trust. If the message I am discerning continues to percolate within, I believe, I embrace, and I act upon that Voice.

God loves you, God loves me, and will make the Divine Voice known. Jesus said, *"My sheep know My Voice."* He seems confident that we'll be able to distinguish the Divine from the human, the Spirit from the flesh, the Angelic from the worldly.

Nothing compares to practice. Test the Voice and see. I have found this to be a most safe principle. How? *"Let peace be the umpire"* notes a particular Bible version in the book of Colossians. Umpires call the game, what's fair and what's foul, strike or ball, in or out. So it is with the Peace of God.

"The Peace that passes understanding" cannot be easily mimicked. True peace becomes the guardian of our hearts and minds against bogus enunciations. Peace is a filter to screen the bad and the wrong from the good and the right.

Sense the serene. Pay attention when it's disrupted. God is in the calm. Listen and you will hear.

Shhh...Listening For God

Listening for God Discussion Questions
Chapter 4 – Hear Ye, Hear Ye, Hear Ye

1. Do you find solitude and silence uncomfortable?

2. Have some of your prayers lost their meaning?

3. When practicing solitude and stillness, do you find that your prayers seem deeper or more meaningful?

4. What is your comfort level when you are alone in silence?

5. Can you tell of an instance where God whispered in your ear and you responded?

6. What are your concerns or expectations if you hear God's Voice?

Chapter Five

THE SPEAKING ABSENCE

Ever stare at a printed 3-D image? I guess the trick is to hold it out from your person at arm's length. Then really, really concentrate your gaze while looking into the scene and slowly pull the object toward your face. At some point, the portrayal is supposed to change from flat to dimensional. It never worked for me.

Imagine taking a picture of the Ark of the Covenant. Surely you have seen Indiana Jones and his sidekick lift the venerated object out of its stone coffin with long wooden rails. What a sight.

You and I can try holding a picture of the Ark at a distance and stare. We can even pull it slowly toward our noses until we are almost cross-eyed. Maybe try the brightly colored red and blue movie theater square papered glasses. Or plastic. The result is always the same. Between the cherubims there is nothing. Just plain void.

The Ark is described in Scripture pretty much as we have seen in Hollywood archaeological backdrops. Two ornamental cherubims

Shhh...Listening For God

spread their wings as they sit looking down upon the lid, *"the Mercy Seat."* Since the lid and the cherubims were made out of one piece of gold, I concede their wings must have touched each other for stability high at the tip of the triangular-shaped vacancy.

However, the Ark itself was made of acacia wood and overlaid with the most precious metal. Constructed of two substances, gold representing deity, and wood representing humanity, the Covenantal Chest portrayed the incarnate nature of the Christ.

On the Day of Atonement, the High Priest sprinkled the sacrificial blood of an animal on the Mercy Seat. Although it was here on the purposely prepared coverture where the blood was applied, the Mercy Seat was the only place to sit and rest had the High Priests been permitted to do so during their ministrations. Since their priestly work was never finished, they never sat. . .until. . .

Imagine the significance of the ascended Christ *"sitting down"* in a state of eternal rest at the right Hand of God, His blood poured out on the Cross once and for all, becoming for us the Mercy Seat of Heaven. The old hymn by Isaac Watts, *At the Cross,* says it well:

Alas! And did my Savior bleed? And did my Sovereign die? Would He devote that sacred head for sinners such as I?

Was it for crimes that I have done He groaned up on that tree? Amazing pity! Grace unknown! And love beyond degree!

Well might the sun in darkness hide, and shut his glories in, When Christ, the mighty Maker, died for man the creature's sin.

But drops of grief can ne'er repay the debt of love I owe:
Here, Lord, I give myself away, 'tis all that I can do!

John the apostle says in his first letter, that Jesus was the *"propitiation,"* literally *"the Mercy Seat,"* for our sins. From the Cross Jesus cried, *"It is finished."* Stated by the author of the book of Hebrews (10:11-14), it reads:

And every priest stands ministering daily and offering repeatedly the same sacrifices, which can never take away sins. But this Man, after He had offered one sacrifice for sins forever, sat down at the right hand of God, from that time waiting till His enemies are made His footstool. For by one offering He has perfected forever those who are being sanctified.

Through Jesus, each of us can be reconciled into relationship with a Holy God. Jesus became the New Temple, which in Pauline language made it possible for our earthly bodies to be temples of the Holy Spirit as well.

So what exactly is the Ark of the Covenant? Sensational speculation has certainly had its heyday depicting the Golden Wonder as anything from a transmitter to a transponder or transporter.

Like other iconic symbols, possibly the Ark is a window for us to see God, or more correctly a special point from which to hear God. For that seems to be the Scriptural determination in the book of Exodus.

Make one cherub at one end, and the other cherub at the other end. . .And the cherubim shall stretch out *their* wings above, covering the mercy seat with their wings, and they shall face one another. . .

Shhh...Listening For God

You shall put the mercy seat on top of the ark, and in the ark you shall put the Testimony that I will give you. And there I will meet with you, and I will speak with you from above the mercy seat, from between the two cherubim which *are* on the ark of the Testimony, about everything which I will give you in commandment to the children of Israel.

Have any of us ever intently inspected the spot from which God speaks? It's a very specific place—from above the lid, from between the winged creatures. But there is nothing there. Absolutely nothing. No image. No tangible depiction. Just space. Empty space at that. At worst, oblivion.

Rowan Williams, an Anglican Bishop, called this blank space *"The great speaking absence."* Were we expecting *"The great speaking Presence?"* I was. The most sacred spot where God was in the midst of a worshipping people appeared to be a vacuum.

By the time of the Babylonian captivity, the Ark of the Covenant had disappeared and has never been found, erased from the pages of history. No matter, the Jews still honored the sacred space where the Ark was once displayed with Temple worship and sacrificial practices. The Holy of Holies, for all intents and purposes, was itself an empty chamber.

In 63 BCE, after conquering the gated city, the Roman General Pompey, demanded the honor of entering the Central Space of fallen Jerusalem, the place which housed the noted God of the Jews. He came out somewhat puzzled, confused over all of the religious fervor that surrounded a seemingly abandoned room. Why here? Why this?

Shhh...Listening For God

Throughout the centuries, the Nation of Israel has celebrated and continues to celebrate many official Feasts, honoring the God of their chosen beginnings. The main Feasts required Jews in Jesus' time to pilgrimage to the Holy City drawing as near to that Sacred Space as possible. And thus, they trekked to the Temple, which had been lavishly rebuilt by Herod.

If you were a devout Jew of the time, preparation was necessary. You would pack your bags, acquire extra cash, secure humped transportation, and so on. Don't forget a sacrifice. *"Are we there yet?"* the children would ask.

You would finally arrive and experience the hustle and bustle of thousands of other wayfarers occupying the already crowded metropolis. You might have to settle for lodging not quite so accommodating, like a cave, since the Innkeeper would inform you *"No vacancy!"*

After a good night's sleep you would make your way to the grand southern staircase leading up to Temple Mount. No running the steps as they were deliberately designed with varying widths and differing heights for the reading of the *Processional Psalms.* It would have been easy to fall on your face in your accelerated approach. But after a quick dip in the *Mikvah,* the ritual cleansing bath, you would be ready to meet your God.

You would make your way through the tumultuous outer courts. A melee of distracting stock market-like buying and selling would fill the air. The squawk of birds, the ruckus of caged animals and the squabbling over Temple currency would lacerate the consecrated sacrarium.

You would have come all this way only to discover that no one was home. There was no Oz-like face behind the inner curtain. No required acts of heroism in order to acquire acceptance by the gods. No captured sinister broomstick trophy necessary. No ding dong song to be sung. No yellow brick road to somewhere.

You would be greeted with space. Sacred yes, even holy. But it was a *"speaking absence."*

When entering the Holy Place from where God speaks, silence is a pre-requisite if one is to hear correctly. Maybe most like noise in their lives because of the consternation about hearing that certain Voice from beyond. Noise is permissible everywhere except when it comes to the spiritually sacred stuff. Sister Jeremy Hall asks:

> What then is real silence? It is a positive receptivity, a creative waiting, a welcoming openness. It is openness to God, to our deepest selves, to others, both as individual persons and as the human community, to beauty and truth and goodness, to mystery – and to the word of Scripture that reveals God, and to the Word Who is God's Son.

No other piece of Temple furniture was like the Ark and the Mercy Seat. From above the lid God dwelt in brightness with an illuminating visible Presence—permanent Light in an otherwise darkened chamber. At the end of the Great Book, the final chapters of Scripture declare we will have no need for the sun or other

Shhh...Listening For God

artificial suppliers of luminescence. God's eternal Presence will be more than enough.

The Hebrews called this manifestation of the visible Glory the *"Shekinah,"* a non-biblical term, but an expression which does show up in Rabbinical writings. The *Shekinah* was the Glory that provided the Israelites with God's guidance, God's protection, God's forgiveness, God's power, and more. Some read it as the *"Cloud"* that rolled in and upon the Gathered Assembly which inhibited the priests from ministering their official duties. The moment ruled then and should now.

As New Testament participants, we can never forget that everything in the Christian Church can become nothing more than empty ceremony and meaningless formality without God's Presence, the *Shekinah*, His Holy, Holy Spirit.

Jesus promised, *"Where two or three are gathered together in My Name, **there am I** in the midst of them,"* a direct reference to the outpouring of the *Shekinah* Glory, the Presence of the Living God.

Let's shift from one Testament to the next. In Hebraic thought, the chamber of the Holy of Holies where God lived in the nothingness between the wings of the cherubims was called *"the Father's House."* Informed with that small detail, watch as we advance from how Moses and others interpreted the *"speaking absence"* to how Jesus understood the sacredness of this designated space. Is

91

Shhh...Listening For God

this why He entered the Temple area with a righteous temper and braided rope?

The Cleansing of the Temple, as we call it, is told in every Gospel: Matthew 21, Mark 11, Luke 19, and John 2. However, the placement of the story early in Johannine thought is unique. John positions the acclaimed event at the beginning of Jesus' ministry rather than at the end as in the Matthean version.

One of the major themes of the Gospel of John is that Jesus is the fulfillment as well as the replacement of all the Jewish Feasts. Read and reap!

As we enter the story we read, *"And the Jews' Passover was at hand, and Jesus went up to Jerusalem."* It was the month of March and the Jews were beginning to enter the Holy City as required. However, we know they were headed toward the *"speaking absence,"* the *"sacred space."* Jesus was going like everybody else, but He saw the scene quite differently than they.

The repetitive persecution of the Jews had dispersed them literally all over the world. So when they would come to the Feasts, the money changers would exchange foreign currency for specific Temple currency, with a little profit margin in the middle—for shipping and handling, a mark up.

"And Jesus found in the Temple those that sold oxen and sheep and doves, and the changers of money sitting." Not a glorious image. But what happened next is considered one of the most radical acts of Jesus in all of Scripture:

92

Shhh...Listening For God

And when He had made a scourge of small cords, He drove them all out of the Temple, and the sheep, and the oxen; and poured out the changers' money, and overthrew the table.

What got into Him? Jesus created a disruptive scene causing infectious pandemonium, especially with the sound of money dancing and dingling across the floor.

Jesus responded to this Temple theft with righteous indignation. Theft is one of the greatest crimes of humankind, if not the greatest. It was violence, *"wrong-doing,"* stated in the Hebrew language as *Hamas,* which brought the flood of Genesis. And according to Isaiah the Prophet, at the end of time, *Hamas* will once and for all be removed from the whole earth.

My Jerusalem friend, A.R. Oz, defines *Hamas* as a union between terror and theft, a composite idea rather than a single term. It is something which gradually corrupts our fellow human beings and ends in utter ruin.

As Jesus approached the Temple area and saw the ruinous activity, the robbery of the poor, the despicable treatment of Holy Ground, He erupted. What's more, the distortion of sacrificial intent had been sanctioned by the Priestly elite. They had made *Hamas* legal in the Temple Courts, within sight and sound of the very God, the Holy One, who occupied their distinguished edifice nearby.

And He said unto them that sold doves, take these things away! Do not make My Father's house a house of merchandise.

93

Jesus' passion for God's House was evident: And His disciples remembered that it was written: *"The zeal of thine House hath eaten me up."* Yet there is something missing in John's narrative that we expect to read since it is scripted everywhere else. Actually, the phrase is quite proverbial: *"You have made it a den of thieves."*

For John, *"the den of thieves"* was insignificant, for he seemed to be using the story for another purpose.

Let me propose that the anger of Jesus in the Cleansing of the Temple was not solely about the dishonesty and thievery of those who sold sacrificial offerings at inflated prices. He was also cleansing the Temple of clamor, clatter, and chatter. Noise! **Jesus was restoring the sanctity of silence.**

The Temple in Jerusalem was the center of Jewish spirituality. It was originally constructed around the concept of *sacred place, silent space.* In this way, God's manifest Presence was present to them. Here they could immerse themselves in the *speaking absence.*

Why did the Temple need cleansing? The reaction of Jesus was to unholy happenings and unholy sounds that infiltrated a space designed for listening. Mother Teresa recorded:

> The fruit of prayer is a deepening of faith. The fruit of faith is love, and the fruit of love is service. But to be able to pray we need silence; silence of the heart. And if we don't have that silence, we don't know how to pray.

Activity in the Temple sent the wrong message regarding spirituality. Jesus corrected that notion in one strong visual sermon. Space and silence are Divine. Create space anywhere—between arching cherubims, between branching trees, between appointments, or between rushing thoughts. God will fill it. God is the *No-thing* that holds everything together. The ultimate scientific goal of discovery is God.

It is tempting to fill space with noise and busyness. Be careful. Crowded church schedules are notorious for looking spiritual.

When was the last time we cleansed our own temples? Saint Paul calls the human body *"a temple of the Holy Spirit."* Have our lives become a bit noisy? Busy perhaps? Hiding from anything? What is being avoided?

Seems simple enough. We honor God by making room and guess what? God will fill it. The *"speaking absence"* becomes the *"speaking Presence"* when we allow the Voice of the Lord to be the one and only Voice heard at the time.

Becoming quiet usually takes some seclusionary effort on my part. I have learned to be still in a crowd, but not quite enough to hear the Voice of God with true clarity. Noise is powerfully distracting.

Entering the biblical prayer closet reinforces the need for muffled surroundings. God's *Speaking Presence* is demonstrated as an experience molded by the hushed interior of the Holy of Holies.

Christians are no longer confined to a specific dimensional expanse. Yet the principle of *Sacred Space* remains the same. If we really want to listen for God, our surroundings make a difference.

Possibly, we should think of dedicating our sense of God's Presence in two ways. Before we think of secluding our external space, we need to consider our internal wishes. By that I mean, our hearts must be desirous of Divine interaction or we may find ourselves unprepared for, even callous to God's manifestation of Transcendence. If we do not desire God's Voice, we will not hear what God desires us to understand.

It is imperative that our yearning for God be pure in intention and sacred in response. If so, we will take the necessary steps to place ourselves in Heaven's haven. And that usually entails a process of preparation.

Surveying the space where we intend to meet God is significant. Often places become sacred after a stirring visitation from the Holy Spirit. But it does not hurt to create a place set apart for prayer in readiness of Divine encounter.

Positioning ourselves for expectation goes a long way to welcoming the Presence of God into our lives. Our actions reveal a seriousness that attracts God in contrast to heedless pride which God resists. We need to humble ourselves.

In the past, I have had to release my expectations and cleanse my setting from unholy intrusions, just like Jesus did. Every so often, our temples must endure a sound scrutiny of prospect and practice. Over time, routines settle in and we find ourselves distant from the very One with whom we covet closeness.

I implore, *"Seek first the Kingdom of God and His righteousness. . ."* What happens after that is astounding! If we're going through the motions of seeking, then we should keep going. Let us

Shhh...Listening For God

simply reframe our perspective. The One who turned plain water into fresh wine will take the ordinary of the habitual and fill it with meaning overflowing.

Place yourself before the Lord. Give God your hands, your feet, your eyes, your heart. Then give your ears. *Listen to what God says.* God is present and is still speaking.

If you seek you shall find. If you listen, you will hear.

Shhh...Listening For God

Listening for God Discussion Questions
Chapter 5 – The Speaking Absence

1. What is significant regarding God speaking from an empty space?

2. How do you react to Mother Theresa's statement, *"if we don't have that silence, we don't know how to pray?"*

3. Where is the center of your spirituality?

4. What are your expectations that you will have to release to prepare yourself for a Holy visit?

5. How might God speak to us in less than optimal situations?

6. What makes something sacred?

Chapter Six

LISTENING TO HEAR

Some time ago I heard a cute story about a grandfather visiting his daughter and son-in-law. After dinner he informed everyone, *"Well, I'm going for a walk."* Like most family members who watch over the *"metal years"* of their parents, they were concerned.

Like the *middle years* of forgetfulness, in the *metal years* of age-fullness, we have silver in our hair, gold in our teeth, and lead in our pants.

"Where are you going, Dad?" *"Just around the block. Don't worry, I'll be back in 20 minutes,"* Grandpa said. Two hours later the house was full of frantic worry. *"Should we call the police?"* All of a sudden Grandpa leisurely came through the squeaky screen door smilin' away. *"Where have you been?"* he was gently scolded. *"Oh, I ran into an old friend and he just wouldn't stop listening."*

Listening is rare, both when it is given and when it is received. Pedagogically, it is a skill. I have often boasted that if I can teach someone to listen, I can guarantee him or her a job or a promotion.

Listening is a lost art these days. Yet, it is essential in all meaningful relationships.

In school we teach reading, writing, and arithmetic. We may periodically offer an elective on communication—polished delivery, bigger words, standing upright. Listening is the neglected piece in critical instruction. Dallas Willard articulates our inability well:

> Why do we insist on talking as much as we do? We run off at the mouth because we are inwardly uneasy about what others think of us. Eberhard Arnold observes: "People who love one another can be silent together." But when we're with those we feel less than secure with, we use words to "adjust" our appearance and elicit their approval. Otherwise, we fear our virtues might not receive adequate appreciation and our shortcomings might not be properly "understood."

This explains why prayer is usually a one-sided monologue—telling God rather than communing with God. Silence with the Divine makes us a bit nervous. Out of fear we end up speaking fast and long, usually lacking in qualitative substance. *Me, me, me, me, me!*

As in the British sitcom, we are *Keeping Up Appearances* with proper speech, appropriate dress, puffed up stories, and name-dropping. I'm sure the God of the universe who "paves streets with gold" is hardly impressed with our verbosity. What does get Divine attention is someone who is willing to look and listen. Elizabeth Barrett Browning states the circumstance well:

Earth's crammed with heaven, and every common bush afire

with God; but only he who sees, takes off his shoes, the rest sit round it and pluck blackberries.

Moses was one who looked and listened. A novel character this Moses, *he is.* As the talk of the Torah reflects, *"So when the LORD saw that he turned aside to look, God called to him from the midst of the bush.. . ."* Taking time to look is no small matter. God is manifesting in places burning with Divine Presence, trying to get our attention. If we are not careful, we might just *walk on by.*

Researchers say we only truly listen to another individual for about 7 seconds. Talk about short attention spans. Just after a few blinks of the eye, we are already planning our response. Talking seems to take precedence, we feel safer talking than listening. Listening means we have to set our self-absorption aside and let the other person have the floor.

In the Small Group Ministry of our church it is not uncommon for us to have a piece of "12 x 12" vinyl tile in the middle of the circle. A simple remodeling discard that matches nothing, belongs to no one. When participants feel they want to speak openly and trustingly, we ask them to pick up the tile. This means *"I have the floor now."* No interruptions permitted. No fixing responses solicited or requested. The group is to actively listen to whomever *"holds the floor."*

Allowing the speakers to freely tell their stories trains the rest of the group in the art of respectful restraint. It's a great experience.

One of the only ways I have found to discover whether or not another person is truly, really, genuinely, sincerely listening—is to see if he or she can say back to me *"This is what I hear you saying."* Without that simple response of active, reflective feedback, they most likely were thinking of themselves and not listening at all.

"Active" implies engagement through such things as eye contact, nodding of the head, leaning forward, and at least a vocal *"uh-huh"* once in awhile. Quaker professor and author, Douglas V. Steere, comments regarding the phenomenal effects of listening. He states:

> In order to listen discerningly to another, a certain maturity is required, a certain self-transcendence, a certain expectation, a patience, an openness to the new. In order to really listen, there must be capacity to hear through many wrappings and only a mature listener, listening beyond the outer layer of the words that are spoken, is capable of this.

The quiet of the night watch is often a time of deep listening and engagement. No longer encumbered by the busyness of the day's activities, we are open in spirit and soul, to hear and receive various impressions.

Thomas Edison used to take naps to induce creative thought. Relaxing in a comfortable recliner, he would hold ball bearings in his hands. On the floor next to his chair were pie tins, positioned under his clenched fists. When he would drift into sleep, he would enter a hypnogogic state, allegedly a creative time of open-mindedness; his hands would relax and drop the metal balls making an awakening noise. Edison would then jot down any innovative thoughts.

Are creative ideas awaiting us, witty inventions that could prosper our lives and propel the Kingdom forward? Sadly, like

Shhh...Listening For God

coloring a printed drawing, we concentrate on keeping expected colors within the lines. As a former art teacher, I could give you a gold star for such tedious efforts. But is that the point? Creativeness often exceeds the lines of expectation. Only God would put orange and heliotrope together for a breathtaking sunset. Don't you want more from life and yourself? I give you permission. Color outside the lines. Think Godlike. Live creatively. Listen carefully.

Meanwhile, back at the church, I think most people pay their tithes so that the minister has to go up into the mysterious smokey mount with all the flashing light and thunderous booms to listen for God instead of them. *"You go and talk to God for us, and then come back and tell us what He said."* Nobody admits pushing the minister forward into the *"hands of an angry God,"* but every Sunday, week after week, it is the same.

Yet God calls out to all, young and old, experienced and immature, prophet, priest, and parishioner. God loves to talk. *Shhh. . .* Our task is to learn to listen.

Michelangelo got it right. When we see the finger of God and the hand of humanity reaching for each other, it is God's Hand doing the straining. The hand of humanity is somewhat limp and lackadaisical. God always has been and always will be the One encouraging relationship and conversation. God yearns to draw us near.

Relationship without communication is a divorce waiting to happen. If we believe God loves us, we can bet God is trying to reach us, attempting at all costs to speak a word of hope to the beloved fiancée of the Divine.

What happens if we do not hear? What happens if we do not obey? In this earthly life being in God's will is hard enough, but being out of God's will could be disastrous.

One of the unique stories in Holy Writ is about a young boy Samuel trying to discern God's Voice. He thought his mentor and spiritual guide, the elder Eli, was calling him in the dark. But we know differently. He was learning to listen for God.

> Now the boy Samuel ministered to the LORD before Eli. And the word of the LORD was rare in those days; *there was* no widespread revelation.
>
> And it came to pass at that time, while Eli *was* lying down in his place, and when his eyes had begun to grow so dim that he could not see and before the lamp of God went out in the tabernacle of the LORD where the ark of God *was,* and while Samuel was lying down, that the LORD called Samuel. And he answered, "Here I am!" So he ran to Eli and said, "Here I am, for you called me." And he said, "I did not call; lie down again." And he went and lay down. Then the LORD called yet again, "Samuel!" So Samuel arose and went to Eli, and said, "Here I am, for you called me." He answered, "I did not call, my son; lie down again."

This precious event took place in a town called Shiloh just north of Jerusalem. It was here that the Land was divided and distributed to the twelve tribes and for the time being, the Ark of the Covenant was resting in a makeshift Temple. The tradition of pilgrimaging to Shiloh once a year had already begun.

Shhh...Listening For God

A woman named Hannah, who was barren, came to Shiloh and prayed to God for the blessing of a child. God heard and responded. She dedicated that child to the LORD and eventually brought the young Samuel to service in the Temple. In the history of Israel, this is considered one of the most exciting periods and contains the accounts of the lives of Samuel, Saul, and David.

Now Samuel did not yet know the LORD, nor was the word of the LORD yet revealed to him.

And the LORD called Samuel again the third time. So he arose and went to Eli, and said, "Here I am, for you did call me." Then Eli perceived that the LORD had called the boy. Therefore Eli said to Samuel, "Go, lie down; and it shall be, if He calls you, that you must say, 'Speak, LORD, for Your servant hears.'" So Samuel went and lay down in his place.

Now the LORD came and stood and called as at other times, "Samuel! Samuel!"And Samuel answered, "Speak, for Your servant hears."

As a young child, Samuel was committed to the Lord. His four-fold reply, *"Here I am"* models the posture needed if we are to hear the Voice of the Divine. There are many voices urgently beckoning for our attention. We should not find it odd that Samuel was having trouble discerning who was calling. All Christians understand this difficulty.

Eli played a significant role. More than representing a passing of the guard, he also represents the essential spiritual guide in each of our lives. We need an experienced someone who can point us to the deeper waters of transformational encounters and help us sort Spirit-talk from self-talk.

Shhh...Listening For God

Samuel's learning to perceive the Voice of God was a step of faith like the one we must all take; lying still, waiting, prayerfully sifting the thoughts of the heart. Then he utters *"Speak, the ears of your servant are open."* How precious this must have been to God.

God is calling out. **When everything is still, God's Voice comes riding the waves of the cool night air.** Like Samuel, we may not always discern rightly the first time, nor even the second. But the elder Eli encouragingly positioned him the third time with awakened senses. Likewise, must ready ourselves the same way.

The *"Confessional Movement"* today would have us alter this text to read *"Listen, LORD, for your servant is speaking,"* putting the emphasis on the tongue. Let us remember that as creatures graced of God's own design, we are always in a listening posture. The biblical emphasis is upon the ear. God remains Sovereign, the One who speaks, the One who calls, the One who answers. Devotional author, Thomas Kelly, sets the tone of our prayers:

> For God Himself works in our souls, in their deepest depths, taking increasing control as we are progressively willing to be prepared for His wonder. We cease trying to make ourselves the dictators and God the listener, and become the joyful listeners to Him, the Master Who does all things well.

Just wait, listen within. God is there. The Omniscient does not take demands from us very well, but will disclose Divine plans and purposes many times over if we will tenderly approach— *"Speak, LORD, for your servant is waiting, waiting and listening."*

Shhh...Listening For God

Harvard scholar, Charles Copeland, was asked one day by a student why there was no class on conversation. *"What can I do to learn?"* The professor said, *"Well, if you'll just listen, I'll tell you."* *"Oh, okay,"* the student replied. After a long awkward pause of silence, the expectant student said to Professor Copeland, *"I...I'm listening."* To which Copeland responded, *"Well, you're learning already."*

When I look back upon my own spiritual journey, I am ever grateful for mature mentors. These men took me by the hand and directed my connection to God and community.

We all need an Eli or two in our lives. **I didn't even know the term *"spiritual guide"* existed in my early days. Nonetheless, I knew I needed to seek out people more experienced in the Faith to bring me along.**

Developing relationships with such individuals is paramount in advancing to maturity. I would not be who I am and where I am without them. Some of these elder types were there for a season, others lasted for decades. Not all of them were skilled in biblical studies, prayer projects, or ministerial expertise. Many were just men who modeled Christian masculinity. One specifically, named Vern Kassouf, helped form my attitudes on leadership and business. I shall never forget him nor his deposit into my life.

What blesses me is that none of them exerted authority over me, nor did they try to exhibit control of my life in any fashion. They served

107

as validating listeners, accountability partners, and frontier guides providing direction now and then through the thick and the thin.

Most importantly, my mentors would not have succeeded in their God-given task had I not submitted myself to their friendships. I believe God surrounds us with the right people to get us where we need to be. Let's admit it. We will not get there by ourselves. We need the experienced, the tried and tested, to give us some valuable pointers.

At my age, I now serve in a mentor capacity, continuing what others have done for me. Yet, I find Heaven is still gracing my life with fresh companions who champion God's Spirit. If we remain open, God supplies us with healthy relationships. As Paul stated, we have *"many instructors but not many fathers."*

To find true sources of spiritual wisdom, we need not look far and wide. Frequently they are closer than we think. And most often they are more than willing to assist. The question remains, are we humble and open enough to allow someone with seasoned senses to speak into our lives?

Americans are adorned with the idea of rugged individualism. So much so that this becomes the standard of maturity. Oddly, the mark of true spiritual refinement is interdependence, not independence. The first sin of the Bible is the thought of going it alone.

I encourage you to prayerfully see if there are some Elis nearby (or Elaines as the case may be), those precious saints who will steer you in the right direction and keep you on the straight and narrow.

Shhh...Listening For God

Give yourself to them. In return, they will give themselves to you many times over. They will teach you to listen and you will find in this, abundant life.

Shhh...Listening For God

Listening for God Discussion Questions
Chapter 6 – Listening to Hear

1. What is your experience with *"active"* listening?

2. When you have been *"heard,"* how did you feel?

3. How do you position yourself to listen for God?

4. Do you have a spiritual mentor? How has he/she been helpful?

5. Do you feel ready to allow someone to speak into your life?

Chapter Seven

BE STILL AND KNOW

My friend Big John and I had just crossed over the Peace Bridge to Canada, when we stopped at Niagara Falls for a rest and a good meal before heading farther up into Quebec. Thoughts and conversation of hooking fish after fish filled our vehicle with excitement and a slight wager on who would net the biggest catch. Our hopes were high.

Usually the weather is fairly cool and ideal for tasty Walleye and ferocious Northern Pike, and now and then some Lake Trout. But on this trip, it turned unusually warm. Extended periods of daylight made the metal boats and surface temperatures hot, too hot, which resulted in bleached shorts and sunburned chests.

The only things biting were black flies. Since there was nothing else to do, we went out earlier and earlier each day trying to use the coolness of morning as an additional lure.

Eventually, catching fish no longer held our interest. John and I kept our lines in the solar heated bathtub-like water, but just drifted through our day talking, telling stories, taking an occasional dip to cool off, or eating pre-packed lunches on some island nearby. There were times we just laid back on our cushions on opposite ends of the 14 foot craft and took in the sights and sounds of nature.

At one point, we both acknowledged how quiet and still it all was. Beautiful blue skies with puffy white clouds called us into a surreal setting where the lake became like a large, flat mirror reflecting the white birch trees amidst the multi-hued green towering pines.

Soon our conversation turned to discussion of the noiseless pleasantness we had taken for granted. It was then we truly listened to the stillness. Oddly, it was also then that we noticed it wasn't really quiet.

Aroused in mind and heart, we became aware of the rich sounds that were with us all along. Somehow in our limited scope, we had not tuned them in: wolves howling, beavers flapping their tails in warning, eagles squalling their distinctive call, and water falling down the mountainside spilling into the lake.

Concentrating on the stillness, we had found another realm. And that realm was telling its story. We had only just begun to hear.

Be still, and know that I am God; I will be exalted among the nations, I will be exalted in the earth!

In Psalm 46, prose portrays a profound truth. Stillness equips. *"Be still"* means to *"leave off, to let go."* Unless the reader sees the value of stillness, however, it is very hard to let go of anything.

Eugene Peterson, in his highly touted contemporary version of the Bible, *The Message*, states it with practical relevance: *"Step out of the traffic!"* Peterson's image of crowded lanes and bumper to bumper busyness seems fitting to what has been called in recent years—the Rat Race.

Years ago, I read a medical report of a doctor and his assistant working with rats. They decided to actually subject the vermin to the *"rat race"* of life that we endure almost daily. In their test, the hairy creatures with wiry tails were jostled about as if riding in a car. The doctor played loud music, honked horns, and introduced the sounds of aircraft.

In a very short time, the blood pressure of the rats had gone through the ceiling. Their irritability was also highly accentuated with an expressed inability to cope. What's more, the doctor and his assistant experienced the same manifestations of elevated blood pressure and noted heightened aggression between colleagues.

The most prominent emotional illness of the 1990s (which has yet to escape us), was technically called *"Compulsivity,"* an addiction to achievement and accomplishment. Many still just simply call it *"Drivenness,"* the insatiable desire to do more and be more.

Add to drivenness the ingredients of perfection and performance, and we will have met the *"applauded addictions"* which characterize the epidemic of deteriorating spiritual and emotional health. Like the disciples themselves, we have *"toiled all night,"* but have come up empty.

In leaving the practice of *"stillness,"* we have switched from human beings to human doings. *"Be still"* is a challenging, biblical concept. Human beings are those people who have a healthy feeling of self-worth and personal value apart from their activity. Human doings are those who have an unhealthy feeling of self-worth and personal value, and thus, feel they have to prove their worth everyday.

Consequently, and it is a consequence, human doings must always be accomplishing, performing, and perfecting. I know all too well. Human doings never find rest.

Believers openly declare that we do not follow the ways of the world, but when the tire meets the road many argue otherwise. The late Catholic mystic, Henri Nouwen, well-known professor and author in modern spirituality declares:

> Just look for a moment at our daily routine. In general we are very busy people. We have many meetings to attend, many visits to make, many services to lead. Our calendars are filled with appointments, our days and weeks filled with engagements, and our years filled with plans and projects. There is seldom a period in which we do not know what to do, and we move through life in such a distracted way that we do not even take the time and rest to wonder if any of the things we think, say, or do are worth, thinking, saying, or doing. We simply go along with the many "musts" and "oughts" that have been handed on to us, and we live with them as if they were authentic translations of the Gospel of our Lord.

Workaholism is rampant today. Staying late at the office, coming in early, working through the weekends are all symptomatic of our current struggle. We have lost our balance. We have lost our way.

Spending time with God means just that. *"Be still and know."* Can we find the time to be with the Divine apart from a spiritual activity? From our current cultural paradigm, to be silent with God without performance may prove to be confusing and unsettling.

Dr. Larry Dossey convinces resistant patients of their *"time sickness"* by asking them to sit quietly, without checking a timepiece or counting, and estimate when a minute has passed. Few wait beyond 20 seconds before indicating *"time's up!"* Their internal clocks are wound so tightly they assume everyone else is running at the same rat race pace.

The race with time has touched me too. I know I have arrived at the state in life where the fast food drive-through is not fast enough. I want my breakfast sandwich and I Want It Now! In my own absorption with time, I think they should limit the number of items any one car can order as in the express checkout at the grocery store!

Perhaps you will, on reflection, recognize the same affliction. Ever count the contents in the shopping cart ahead? *Hey! Hey! They're over the ten item limit!* We have become the math patrol.

I've had the same irritable feelings at the ATM. In my mind, they were not designed for someone to do all their weekly banking at the same time. Enter your PIN, select what you need and quickly get on with it. Everything else should be taken inside the bank. It's my turn. Move on.

It gets worse. We wait again while they put everything neatly away before pulling their vehicles slowly forward. Shouldn't they pull forward and then file their treasury receipts? My time is ticking away, or is that an internal bomb I hear? Can you say conniption?

Constitutionally, we have been guaranteed the right to pursue happiness, and yet we are some of the unhappiest people on the planet. We are also some of the most restless. I'm not referring here merely to RLS, Restless Legs Syndrome, it's much broader than that. Many experience the disruptive disturbance of a cluttered soul. I would call it RLS for sure, Restless Lives Syndrome.

Our nighttime sleeping aid products are as numerous as our fruits and vegetables.

Even so, we wrestle through the night with our thermosoft, memory foam, cervical orthopedic pillows and our satin-edged, fleeced-lined, temperature controlled, heated, security blankets nicely stretched on a comfort select, dial-a-mattress sleep number: firm, medium or cushiony.

Possibly our evening retirement is too silent, too quiet. Perhaps it is the stillness that keeps us awake rather than the caffeine.

Trust is necessary if we are to *"Be still and know."* Faith is required if we are to properly rest. Psalm 46 is a context of conflict. *"Be still"* can be a shout into the chaotic, not all that different from Jesus standing up and facing the torrential storm on the Sea of Galilee.

If the Bible is the guide-Book we claim it is, inspired and authoritative, its message is for every age. The timeless blessing of Holy Writ is that it is organic and always relevant, speaking afresh to every new generation. Scripture calls us to deeper rest and deeper knowing.

Can knowing come from stillness? I believe we are over-informed and under-transformed. At the touch of a button, more knowledge is available today than ever before. However, knowledge in a cognitive sense has seldom solved any of our problems. The human brain is 5% thinking and 95% feeling.

Over the years, the solution to personal dilemma was pulpitized as *"My people are destroyed for lack of knowledge."* Spiritual knowledge (again in a cognitive sense) became the *crème de la crème* answer for problems, conflicts, difficulties, and break-throughs. More Bible knowledge acquired equaled more personal power to overcome. As one who holds multiple degrees, forgive my proclamation, please, I find knowledge over-rated. As Paul dictates in his Corinthian correspondence, *"Knowledge puffeth up."*

God is beyond full knowing. God's infinite, we're finite. God is transcendent. The closer we get to God, or the farther we go into God, the more profound *theologia* becomes. We expect clarity, but we are greeted with ever more mystery.

Mystery comes from the term *myein*, to close, to shut, perhaps the eyes or the lips. With lament, Don Henley of the Eagles sings *"The more I know the less I understand, all the things I thought I knew I'm learning again."*

God's magnitude increases proportionately with study. Enlightenment merely places us in a position to see more, to hear more, to learn more. The journey into the unknown does not create doubt, it creates assurance and a renewal of faith. God is bigger than our limited

Shhh...Listening For God

understanding. God exceeds the breadth, and length, and depth, and height of our comprehension. God is beyond our wildest imagining.

Hosea's declaration, *"My people are destroyed for lack of knowledge,"* was not aimed at the parishioners of his time as it is today. His target was the leaders.

For decades, I have listened to emotionally charged sermons scolding the audience to *"Get into the Word," "Quote Scripture," "Dig into the Book;" "Increase your knowledge and you will increase your blessings."*

Howbeit, the knowledge of which the prophet speaks is not to be found in cerebral complexity or intellectual apprehension of repetitional tidbits. The knowledge of God extends beyond cognitive awareness of biblical detail or prescribed dogma.

Within the Hebrew noun for knowledge, *"da'at,"* lies a verbal stem that includes sexual intimacy in its wider range of meaning. God is seeking from us, spiritual romance. Knowledge constitutes a relationship of the whole person with God that involves feeling as well as thinking. *"Adam knew Eve his wife; and she conceived."*

We ardently embrace *orthodoxy*—right believing. Even defend it. We strongly acknowledge *orthopraxy*—right doing. Even define it. Shouldn't we passionately welcome *orthopathy*—right feeling? We typically deny it.

Walking by faith does not mean ignoring feelings or denying them altogether. We are to walk with our feelings. If four-fifths of

Shhh...Listening For God

the human personality is emotionally based, we should surrender our whole selves to God.

Where leaders have lost touch with the *mysterium tremendum,* God is often reduced to verbal formulamatic operations. Dallas Willard correctly asserts, *"If we can't be transformed we settle for being informed, or worse, conformed."* As always, leaders and priests are responsible for the traditions, practices, and doctrines their congregations will enunciate and enact.

Hosea points the problems in the pew back to where they originated—the pulpit. It was the hierarchy who lacked *"the knowledge."* The people were innocent victims. Ouch. O, help me God.

And the glory of the LORD rested on Mount Sinai, and the cloud covered it six days. And the seventh day He called to Moses out of the midst of the cloud.

Exodus 24:16

Why did God make Moses wait for six days before He spoke? Many of us would have departed days earlier assuming God wasn't going to talk. Most likely, God gave Moses the time he needed to clear his mind and heart. How long does it take for us to unclutter our preconceptions in order for the Divine Voice to become clear?

When Ronald Reagan was running for President, he heard a woman named Juanita Booker sing at one of the many stops on the road. She was an unknown housewife, a mother of five. While traveling the rigors of the campaign trail, Reagan was deeply touched by her ministry of song and said, *"If I get elected, I want you to sing at the inauguration."*

Millions of people watched as this relatively unknown artist stirred the hearts in our country with a soulful rendition of the Star Spangled Banner. With cameras rolling, the media swarmed the event like flies to raspberry jam. Of course, they interviewed her and her wide-eyed children about their mother's new found fame in Washington, D.C.

Juanita said, *"Well, I sing around the house all the time."* But one of the boys spoke up: *"I've always heard you sing, but this is the first time we've really listened."*

There is an interesting term called *monolingualism*. It means we have grown accustomed to hearing only voices like our own. Actually, we insist everyone speak like us as if English is the one true language of the earth. Anything else sounds like the mumbled *blah, blah, blah* of a grown-up in a Charlie Brown Christmas special. We just don't understand the words.

I have met many individuals who are outraged when a clerk in a store (or a waiter, or waitress) speaks with a foreign accent. As citizens of the United States of America, they demand lucid speech from everyone else who lives here. Broken verbiage requires from us, who are Nation-born-inhabitants, more intentional listening, even some interpretation.

Somewhere we have adopted the notion that all people within the *"Land of the Free"* flawlessly speak our confusing system of nouns, verbs, participles, and prepositions. Where this is clearly not the case, I have seen people so angrily frustrated over the laborious

Shhh...Listening For God

interchange that they request another attendant, or with pout in tow, leave the establishment altogether.

Remember my older brother Dennis? He is a regular at the local coffee shop, Amy Joy Donuts on the corner of Richmond and Mayfield, in an eastside suburb of Cleveland. It is a club of mixed characters who meet for their morning brew—lawyers, craftsmen, landscapers, and so on.

Dennis endearingly shared with me about one such person who is deaf. Quietly the man sat sipping his java while others chit-chatted about the NBA or the ongoing yearly NFL quarterback controversy of the constantly shifting Cleveland Browns. Hey, how about those Cleveland Indians?

My brother, in an act of inclusive kindness, subsequently went to a bookstore and purchased a manual on sign language. Rather than forcing the hearing impaired to learn the art of lip reading, Dennis took a step into a new and unexplored world and studied how to display a greeting to those who often have to sit in auditory seclusion.

Imagine the smiled surprise on the face of the lone sipper at the long, stool'd counter when Dennis' simple hand gesture entered his world, breaking the tacit barrier. Fellowship.

God, who sits in the eternal now, waits for the opportunity to interject spiritual *"signs"* into the fervid schedule of our daily routines. Silence may be a relatively novel idea in a shake'n rattle society, where babble is the norm and fanfare the standard of fraternity. In the biblical sense, *being still* puts the *silenteer* in an acute

Shhh...Listening For God

stance of *knowing*.

Being still is not easy. We live in a fidgety world. How often have we stepped out of a line because it was moving too slowly? Driving on the interstate, cars weave dangerously in and out of lanes trying to get ahead of others by mere seconds. Break lights flash with musical syncopation. It's particularly ironic when we all arrive at the exit pretty much at the same time as we sit eagerly waiting in single file for the light to change. *Green, go!*

Being still is a continuing challenge. It is hard enough to slow down, but to stop? Come on. Stillness requires an adjustment and will not happen quickly. It will not happen at all unless we see its importance and we embrace and practice it.

Stillness for me now is most enjoyable. At first, it was like water torture. I would seek other models of connecting with movement and sound, yet I always returned here for true contentment and inner rest. For a workaholic, this is monumental.

Being still can be one of the greatest of spiritual ventures. In no other discipline are we exposed to so many interruptions. It's amazing at what happens around us and in us. Seemingly everything fights our will to be still. Mastering the discipline of silence will take practice.

Because of the numerous assaults on our stillness, the distracted are often tempted to leave off before ever experiencing the knowing. Stay with it. Stillness invites the Divine Presence like no other discipline.

Shhh...Listening For God

Stillness deepens the soul. Stillness uplifts the spirit. Stillness heals the anxious mind. Stillness cures the troubled heart. Stillness is where God is. Stillness is where God meets us. I beseech — be still. The experiential *"knowing"* that comes from those intimate soothings penetrates our innermost, our core longings. Stillness educates far beyond college challenges.

Do you want to learn to *be still?* You will need to pick a spot where you won't be interrupted. *Good luck.* Light a candle. Hold something like a small wooden cross. Then close yourself off and relax within.

Next, sanctify the stillness with a prayer. Practice patience. You will have to disperse a vast array of mindless wanderings about things you ought to be doing. Let each of these thoughts go as quickly as they come. Remember, you have chosen wisely, you have chosen the greater good.

Be fully present to God, *"Be still and know." Shhh. . .* It's God's turn to speak to you. You must never forget, ever, that God came from Heaven to earth and back again just to be with you and me. A new and open lifeline of *tell-all-communication* has begun.

In the Name of Jesus.

Shhh...Listening For God

Listening for God Discussion Questions
Chapter 7 – Be Still and Know

1. Have you had an opportunity to experience the *"silence"* of nature? What do you think about this experience?

2. Why is the practice of stillness so uncomfortable in our society?

3. How can you slow down your day and get out of the *"rat race?"*

4. Can you describe a time when you were the heart and hands of God in the world by including others in your circle of relationships?

5. Where are the places or times in your day where you can be still to allow God to refresh your spirit?

Chapter Eight

FROM PRIVATE SILENCE TO PUBLIC SHOUT

In the fall of 1976, I answered the call of God to enter ministry. For me, being in front of an audience was not new or scary as it is for so many. Entertaining people had been my former lifestyle, only now the method, the model, and the subject matter had shifted to something sacredly significant. After decades of preaching weekly, I still tremble in holy awe as I influence lives caught in the struggle of daily living.

Just in my late 20s, I journeyed west to attend a fairly new school opening in Tulsa, Oklahoma—Rhema Bible Training Center. Having lived on the cultured East coast, I was unprepared for the shock of meeting real Cowboys and Indians. Old covered wagons were long gone, but they had been replaced by pick-up trucks with gun racks, still roaming the wind blown, tumbleweed clad prairies.

Here in the Wild West, the cultural bias of white versus black was simply traded for white versus red. Human depravity is always apparent, only the shade of our cultural sheath changes. We need

Shhh...Listening For God

help. The message of Dr. Martin Luther King's proclamation continues to ring true: *We must arrive at the place where we discern one another by the character of our soul, and not the color of our skin.*

Rhema had now settled in Broken Arrow, a Tulsinian suburb, and was in its third year of operation. Kenneth Hagin was the founder of Rhema. His message of faith in God stirred people, especially those searching for a fresh manifestation of the Spirit to replace the stale routines of church as usual.

Many consider Hagin's message of positive confession extreme. But as someone who spent time with him and his family and approached the fadish doctrine with appropriate filters (like study, reason, prayer, and other commentators), I found Hagin, a former Assembly of God pastor, to be fairly orthodox. I cannot attest to those who took his simple presentation *"to believe"* and magnified it many times over *"to claim."* Hagin was healed from a grave affliction by expressing faith in God's Word. He then proclaimed that model for others to follow. Jesus is the Word made flesh, so to confess written inspired Text is to connect with God through the very Person of Jesus Christ, the Living Word.

The underlying principle here is psychologically sound. If one is to end self sabotage, it is necessary to alter thoughts and speech patterns. Otherwise, constant negativity will feed the villainous toxicity and trap the pawn in fatal self-imprisonment. Paul did well to tell young Timothy that he should be about *"instructing those that oppose themselves."*

Shhh...Listening For God

The Principle of Observer Participancy, noted science theory, teaches that the observer becomes a part of what he or she observes, and in fact creates it. In Dr. Paul Pearsall's language, *"We either make a mess or a miracle of our own life depending on the meaning we choose to give to our living."*

An old medical adage says, *"It matters less what type of disease the patient has than what type of patient has the disease."* Hence, the *"observer"* is a participant in and partial creator of what is observed. Our words, like no other part of us, clearly reflect what we observe, what we believe, and thus what we will conclude.

Science and spirit are not that far apart. Don't be fooled. Our existence is a complex complement of various contributions, from various sources.

Hagin was a master at correcting the damaging destructiveness of that *"little member"* which *"boasteth great things,"* the tongue. He realized, as Scripture teaches, *"the power of life and death"* lies within our daily conceptual utterances. It would be hard to find a doctor who would disagree with this assessment.

On to Bible school. Moving as the May family, pulling a small rented trailer, we arrived in the country western town of legendary *Okies*. We rented an apartment across from the campus and shortly thereafter looked for part-time employment. Classes ran from 8:00 a.m. to 12:00 noon; part-time work would easily fit in to our strictly scheduled lifestyle.

Shhh...Listening For God

We felt we needed to get acquainted with our new homestead, so on a typical steaming hot day, we all piled into our maroon-colored Oldsmobile and drove the city streets just lookin'. My wife was driving, as I was reaching over the vinyl barrier, tending to our two young boys in the back seat.

As we passed a silk screen establishment, silk screening being the kind of work similar to what I had just left in Cleveland, we commented simultaneously, *"Let's note that address so I can come back and put in an application."* At that second, the Holy Spirit spoke to me within and said, *"Stop and go in now."*

"Another test in personal obedience," I thought, and I shared with my spouse what I believed the Lord had uttered. She looked at my attire. *"You don't seem appropriately dressed for an interview."* *"I know,"* I replied, *"but I feel I need to obey the Voice of the Lord."* So we turned around and I went in. There was no receptionist, just a couple of people sitting on a bench. I sat down on the end next to everyone else. I watched a man come out of an adjacent room and depart through the front door. A voice from inside the office yelled, *"Next."* The person on the end got up and went in and everybody else scooted down. I followed along.

Now I was close enough to hear the murmurings from inside. To my amazement, they were interviewing individuals for a new position in the company. I patiently waited my turn and was the last to enter the concealed chamber. A gentle bald headed man with glasses sat behind a desk, *"How may I help you?"* *"I don't know,"* I said.

128

"I was just driving by and the Holy Spirit told me to stop." "Who told you to stop?" he chokingly stammered with a dazed look. *"The Holy Spirit,"* I responded.

I'll never forget the next moment. He got up, went over and closed the door and came back and sat down. With propped elbows and both hands supporting his face, he leaned forward and said, *"Tell me more."* And I did.

It turned out that my inquisitive employer-to-be was a born again Baptist believer and the term *"Holy Spirit"* had caught his attention. *"Are you sure you didn't know I was interviewing?"* He wasn't looking for part-time help, but he could not seem to shake the notion that something Divine was happening between us. *"Let me call you tonight,"* he said. *"I have to think about this."*

I went on my way trusting that God was providentially involved. That evening, my Baptist connection called and said, *"I don't know what to do. Did you find a job yet?" "No,"* I replied. *"Well then, don't go look for one. If I don't hire you myself, I'll find you a job in the city since I know all the printers."*

"This covenant living is too much," I thought to myself. In the morning, this reverent businessman called me again. *"I don't need part-time help, but I'm going to hire you."* I was employed!!

After one week of working at the plant, he gave me my own key saying *"Make your own hours, as many as you want."* He then fired his cleaning crew and hired me to sanitize and scrub the offices. And I did as unto the LORD to the best of my ability.

Shhh...Listening For God

My income for extra services exactly covered my tuition each month. There's more. He would sneak me turkeys and hams at holidays, even bonuses. *"Don't tell the other employees; I'm not supposed to cater to the part-timers."*

Besides blessing me, he hired a friend in the ensuing years and wrote a check which paid off his entire tuition bill at the same Training Center. By the way, my friend knew nothing of the printing industry. He often testified, *"Neal, he hired me because of you."* *"No, I believed he hired you and me because of the Holy Spirit."*

My stay in Tulsa lasted only a year, but the relationship endured for many, many more. This precious man, in time, donated thousands of dollars to my church and ministry. When he retired, he tithed a large sum to the Bible school on behalf of two pastors from Ohio, my friend and me, who had influenced his life. To God be the glory!

The Kingdom of God was advanced fiscally and this Charismatic pastor was blessed beyond measure by a gracious Baptist, serendipitously named Paul, who equally loved and listened to God's Spirit.

How powerful coincidence becomes if we listen for God's Voice. God's promptings can be so slight. We must be careful not to write off the smallest thoughts, inner sense, or Voice that hails from within, *"Stop and go in now."*

The Spirit of God may ask you to write a note, make a call, go for a visit, greet, give, or offer a word of encouragement. All actions done in the Divine Name provide untold felicity for all involved.

Shhh...Listening For God

Lives can be saved, ministries supplied, blessings showered, if we would but be *"Led by the Spirit."*

I have found the leading of the Holy Spirit to be astonishingly practical. Let's do what God says. Test the notion when in doubt. See where the Spirit takes us. Miracles happen. Often they are simple in nature. Yet God is anxious to bless, whether in small or great ways.

Listening is a common Testamental theme. As it starts the beginning of the Old, it starts the beginning of the New. As demonstrated in the Gospels, Jesus practiced this ancient art and honed it as part of His daily devotion to hear, to pray, to proclaim.

The Gospel of Matthew leads the New Testament for a reason. Its ordered structure made it easy to use in the catechism of the early church, instructing converts in the ways of the Lord. This Gospel account can be divided into five sections, thus paralleling it to the first five books of the Old Testament, the Pentateuch, becoming a bridge between the Testaments.

Matthew's Gospel was a new genre, for a new People with a new Law—love God, love one another. . .even your enemies. The vertical element (love of God) and the horizontal element (love of neighbor) reflect the sign of the Cross. It is a cruciform pattern.

While many believe the Cross is a New Testament icon of discipleship, the symbol is, in fact, witnessed throughout Scripture from Genesis to Revelation. The encampment of Israel around the Tabernacle was cruciform, as was the layout of the articles within the Tabernacle.

Shhh...Listening For God

Just think, when Moses looked down from the Holy Mount, he saw thousands of tents, each tribe camped in its designated location. But the overall pattern was cruciform. Since Jesus is the Lamb slain from the foundation of the world, perhaps we shouldn't be so shocked at the minute details of Creator God who shaped the Cosmos with *"intelligent design."*

Joe Eszterhas, my next door neighbor and respected friend, has inspired many with his reverent procession of the Cross in the Holy Angels Church nearby. In his book *Crossbearer*, he tells with honest humor and confessional transparency about his journey from *"Hollywood Animal"* to servant of Christ.

The *"emblem of suffering and shame"* has a way of piercing even the hardest of hearts. With amazing grace, the story of God's forgiving love eventually wears thin the defensive walls of the resistant.

When Joe hit bottom with throat cancer, he called out to his God of childhood memories. Where you ask? Church? Sacrarium? No. It happened on the very streets that intersect our neighborhood. This was certainly not the most sanctified of places to the local passerby with large green garbage cans with black-hinged lids being still wheeled out to the curb every Monday, even for the successful and famous.

In the midst of a typical day, in a most untypical place, the God of Heaven heard Joe's plea and responded. Joe received his miracle. First a new life in Christ and the Church, and second, the restoration of his sickened flesh.

Shhh...Listening For God

Oh, that old rugged cross, so despised by the world, Has a wondrous attraction for me; For the dear Lamb of God left His glory above To bear it to dark Calvary.

In that old rugged cross, stained with blood so divine, A wondrous beauty I see, For 'twas on that old cross Jesus suffered and died, To pardon and sanctify me.

Paul maintains that we are to *"preach Christ crucified,"* an unfaltering presentation of what Jesus accomplished *"in His flesh on the tree."* Whenever forgiveness of sin is questioned by a doubting mind, just look to Golgotha's Hill. There you will see it standing erect, rising up out of the earth almost as if it had been planted. It is the Cross of Christ that binds us to God.

Have you read about Laminins yet? They are a family of structural proteins in the human body which hold us together. They are cell adhesion molecules, the glue which keeps one cell of our body connected to the next. Without them we would, literally, fall apart.

If you'll search the Net or look it up in medical literature, the Laminin icon will appear. It is a cross. It is also trinitarian in nature. What holds each of us together is the biological presence of cross after cross after cross placed throughout the intricate physical specimen called in plain terms—human. *"I will praise You, for I am fearfully and wonderfully made."*

In Matthew Chapter Ten, Jesus echoes what has been said over and over to this point: Creator speaks, creature listens—then we can talk. Any verbalization prior to a listening encounter, is usually tainted with thoughts of self and self-interest no matter how

Shhh...Listening For God

eloquent. God must have the first word and the last word. Silence provides such an opportunity. I paraphrase from collected versions:

What I say to you in the dark you must repeat in broad daylight; What you hear whispered in your ear you must shout from the housetops.

Jesus would tell His disciples in private, things to which the masses were not privy. . .explanations, details, answers to the perplexing, and most significantly, the offer of intimacy. Personally, I would find myself excited and anxious to be that close to the Son of God.

Ever been with someone such as a psychiatrist, prophet, or a mystic, when you feel they can look right through you? It's an awkward moment when you realize they may be analyzing your body language, facial expressions, quirks, and vocabulary. It's only the loving-kindness of Jesus, that non-judgmental demeanor of His, that draws His disciples ever closer.

The promise of Jesus, *"to whisper in the ear,"* repeats that which we have heard all along—God talks, God tells. However, the revelatory breakthrough in the Matthean context is where and how and what He will tell us.

"What I tell you in the dark and/or in secret," calls for a special place and a sacred time in which we withdraw enough to hear the whisper of His Voice. To be sequestered ends up being problematic, however, if our souls are too cluttered with other matters which may weigh heavily upon us. As a result, we will have heard nothing and we will have nothing to shout.

134

Shhh...Listening For God

We can praise the Lord and rant all we like. But what I surmise Jesus is saying is that we may be shouting praise, quoting Scripture, claiming promises as if the emotional elements of volume and repetition will somehow convince us of their truthfulness.

Vibration on the ear always comes before proclamation by the mouth. Hearing in secret always comes before speaking in public. Such knee bending, head bowing practices of listening hone our experiences and careful study with theological accuracy. Moreover, they direct true praise upward to God, rather than feed selfish pride and contribute to a false notion of spiritual elitism, errors which the New Testament writers fought in every letter.

Soli Deo Gloria. All Glory be to God.

We cannot shout another's shout, at least not with any heartfelt passion. If we are going to survive the temptations of the world, we will need to hear God's Voice for ourselves. Vain attempts at makeshift spasmodic stimulants of joyful noise will not last. Knowing the Voice of the Good Shepherd settles the issue of God's existence, God's guidance, and God's purposes, once and for all.

Some years ago, I rented a car and went on a European vacation. Driving on the left side of the road with a steering wheel on the right side of the car proved to be challenging. Spontaneous actions and reactions invariably took me into the path of oncoming traffic. Those Brits can surely get excited! I assure you that they're not as stale and stoic as we have been told.

Shhh...Listening For God

My plan was simple. . .drive back roads, stay off the crowded streets, be careful slinging out of the roundabouts, visit every castle, cathedral, church, and monastery I could find. The border between Scotland and England was lined with time-worn, lattice-like structures portraying monastic life in its prime.

Heading south, I made it a point to see the remains of Glastonbury Abbey, a Benedictine shrine. Glastonbury is in many respects a peculiar place. I thought I had stepped back in time to Haight-Ashbury in the *"Love Period"* of the San Francisco hippie years. It was a time when crystals, beads, long hair, tie-dyed shirts, dancers, and prancers lined the streets.

Glastonbury Abbey is not only a Christian site, but also a magical mystery tour of religious trends of Merlin and the tales of King Arthur.

Walking the grounds where it is believed that Joseph of Arimathea brought the chalice of Christ, the Holy Grail, was romantically moving. Little is left of the buildings and chapels, a wall here and there and some weathered remains of monastic life. But the prayerful Presence of God's Spirit lingers ever true.

In a museum-type building, historical artifacts and information regarding the site are displayed. Visitors can try his or her artistry at colored rubbings on heavy black paper over assorted brass religious representations. Artifacts are exhibited creatively and the rules of Saint Benedict are colorfully painted on scroll-like depictions of scribal friars with their feathered quills dipped in ink.

Shhh...Listening For God

One such Benedictine tenet stands out: *"There are times when good words are to be left unsaid out of esteem for silence."*

Wherever you go, the message of the ancients is unchanging — people who have discerned the pathway to God always come through the exfoliating gauntlet of pure and total silence. From out of the silence true "shouts" are birthed.

The Matthean *"shout"* of which Jesus speaks is a proclamation of freedom. Freedom from sinful self, freedom from the burden of toxic shame. Quite often this is the reinforcement we will hear when we enter the secret chamber of private audience.

Here in total seclusion, God re-affirms unconditional love for us, God's grand forgiveness, and God's bountiful grace, as we wrestle with the thoughts of who we are and what we may have done. Typically, it is the broken, beaten-down self we initially hear. Once we are assured of God's mercy over our darkened souls, we re-emerge with new selves, brightened by the touch of *Amazing Grace*.

Our shout is one of confident joy. Our shout is one of fuller understanding and of gracious love. To those who dare enter the quiet silence, judgmentalism is finally squashed. Prejudice is no longer an issue.

Private silence dramatically influences public shout. To the ear trained in seclusion, God whispers Divine pleasure, but also Divine guidance.

Have you evaluated the ratio of noise to silence in your life? Go ahead. What did you find out? I thought so. Private silence is lacking

Shhh...Listening For God

in most of our lives. It's time to change the weekly schedule, the daily routine of flaming fervor in favor of fanning quietude.

Public shouts are rather shallow if not preceded by time with God. Find a private place. Give God private time. As Christ did with His twelve, I'm sure He will do for us. He will share the most intimate things, things only for the attentive and the available. These understandings are reserved for His lovers and friends. *Try it, you'll like it.*

Shhh...Listening For God

Listening for God Discussion Questions
Chapter 8 – From Private Silence to Public Shout

1. How has your behavior changed since encountering the Divine Voice?

2. In what ways are you lover and friend of Jesus?

3. If you *"You cannot shout another's shout,"* how do you go about getting your own *"shout?"*

4. The author contends that people who have discerned the pathway to God have done so through total silence. If that is so, how do you follow that example?

5. Is private silence lacking in your life? Why?

Chapter Nine

QUIET PLACES – SACRED SPACES

"And Jesus withdrew Himself into the wilderness, and prayed." If we haven't been to the Land called Holy, then we have missed experiencing what the Jews call the *"Fifth Gospel."* It proves difficult to interpret the other four Gospels with accuracy without the visual insight of the *"Fifth."*

I have been privileged to tour the *"Fifth"* many, many times. I stood in the very wilderness Jesus chose to enter for prayer. Looking out over this uninhabitable wasteland, I have had to scratch my head and wonder why He would come here.

The wilderness of Judea is barren. Rock and sand, hills and valleys—rarely is there water or anything green or appealing for that matter. If we wander too far away from guides and jeep-like vehicles, one may be lost for quite a long time. Everything looks the same. Confusion quickly sets in causing disorientation that may prove fatal, especially if not enough water has been consumed.

Why would Jesus pick such a place to pray? Padded kneelers would be fine, or even the cool shade of a garden, but a desert? Hopefully, we might find a cave for relief from the intense heat and a *wadi* (dry river bed) that may still have some standing water.

What is startling about the Lukan assertion that *"Jesus withdrew Himself,"* is the verb tense. From the tense we know He did this on a regular basis. What did He discover there that would pull Him back again and again to something we would easily call *"Godforsaken?"*

Early in His ministry, Jesus heard *"a Voice from Heaven."* I told you God talks. God confirms to Jesus relational pleasure, and immediately after this ecstatic affirmation, it is said, *". . .the Spirit driveth Him into the wilderness."* It almost reads as if Jesus dug His heels in, but was forced to go where He did not want to be.

After all, that is the definition of obedience isn't it? The willingness to be led to where we do not want to go. Like the melodic vocal sensitivity of the old Doris Day song, *Sentimental Journey—* we gotta take that Sacramental Journey, Sacramental Journey home, and go with the flow.

Noted author Ruth Haley Barton clarifies the wilderness, this sea of shimmering sand, as something unique. Much more than blinding minuscule particles of dust or disrupting pebbles infiltrating one's footwear, the desert reaches out like an extended hand of welcome. She expresses:

Shhh...Listening For God

The invitation to solitude and silence is just that. It is an invitation to enter more deeply into the intimacy of relationship with the One Who waits just outside the noise and busyness of our lives. It is an invitation to communication and communion with the One Who is always present even when our awareness has been dulled by distraction. It is an invitation to the adventure of spiritual transformation in the deepest places of our being, an adventure that will result in greater freedom and authenticity and surrender to God than we have yet experienced.

That's why it is here, in the wilderness, that Jesus defeats the Tempter. That initial victory taught Jesus the keys to success. By success, I do not mean fancy clothes, big houses, nice cars, and personal airplanes.

The wilderness strips away all of our stereotypical identity props marking our achievement or status. Everything we use to get through our day—swanky appearance, cyber-collectibles, titles and initials, matching shoes and bag, power suits and colored ties—are of little value in the desert. Henri Nouwen describes the scene in his book, *The Way of the Heart*:

In solitude I get rid of my scaffolding: no friends to talk with, no telephone calls to make, no meetings to attend, no music to entertain, no books to distract, just me—naked, vulnerable, weak, sinful, deprived, broken—nothing. It is this nothingness that I have to face in my solitude, a nothingness so dreadful that everything in me wants to run to my friends, my work, and my distractions so that I can forget my nothingness and make myself believe that I am worth something.

It takes the simplicity of solitude and silence to fortify the soul in order to withstand the onslaught of worldliness. Jesus mixes a series of spiritual practices to recover as the second ADAM all that the first Adam had lost.

Solitude—go into the wilderness. There is nothing, there is no one, only God and the seeking pilgrim. *Silence*—praying to God involves more listening, less speaking. *Simplicity*—fasting allows clear delineation between what is Divinely strategic and what is substanceless aggrandizement of the world.

Today's dazzling and chic Sunday morning church presentations only seem to add to our spiritual dilemma. Great seats for a great show, with great coffee, make the Sabbath mandate a pleasing and comfortable shopping experience. That's how most people find a local faith community.

Like a consumer looking for the best deal for the tithe, we find the church with the most programs and the most comfort, a far cry from the lonely, sun bleached, non-air conditioned, rock hardened arena in the middle of nowhere.

It is no wonder that pastor and parishioner, monk and hermit alike, consider these isolating disciplines of solitude, silence, and simplicity, as the most radical of spiritual practices. Dallas Willard rather pointedly assumes the reason:

> . . .To be in solitude is to choose to do nothing. For extensive periods of time. All accomplishment is given up. Silence is required to complete solitude, for until we enter quietness, the world still lays hold of us. When we go into solitude and

Shhh...Listening For God

silence we stop making demands on God. It is enough that God is God and we are His. We learn we have a soul, that God is here, that this world is "my Father's world.".

What many find confusing is that if Jesus were such a loner, spending so much down time with God in the wilderness, how did He do so much effective ministry for others?

"And Jesus returned in the power of the Spirit." His times of solitude, silence, and simplicity filled Him to overflowing. No wonder so many of us run emotionally thin. Rarely, if ever, do we take the time to find an appropriate place for these Divine encounters, encounters which would empower us.

When stressful situations arise, we lack the proper strength to deal with that which pecks away at our spiritual health of love and patience, faith and hope, joy and kindness. The fruit of the Spirit is absent from our spiritual tree. We are no longer planted near rivers of living water.

It seems paradoxical that time away from others and activities actually invigorates us for activities and others. Kathleen Norris describes the life of an esteemed monk who practiced the very way of Jesus:

...Pilgrims visiting the ancient monasteries of the Egyptian desert could easily pick out the venerable Anthony in a crowd of monks, for this man who was renowned as a hermit literally glowed with hospitality. His life of prayer in solitude had rendered him visibly open and welcoming to others.

145

Shhh...Listening For God

Being with God fills us full of God's Spirit. And there is plenty to go around. Are you and I running on empty? Mere fumes? A desert can be for us anywhere, anytime, chosen or imposed. But the Divine purpose is always the same.

Consider Moses, the greatest prophet of the Testaments. He had reached the highest level of spirituality humanly achievable. Moses spoke with God. Not once, but countless times. He communed with the Divine in the *"Tent of Meeting,"* the supreme goal of many spiritual leaders and followers alike.

Unfortunately, Moses' greatest asset became his greatest liability. Moses lived his spiritual life removed from the masses. According to Rabbi Riskin, God was telling Moses that the goal of religious experience must not be merely Divine intra-action, but also human inter-action.

It's now clear. The *"heavy speech"* of Moses was not a tongue which necessarily stammered, but one which spoke only of theology and law, morality and ethics. He had no time for what we simply call *"fellowship."* His long distance leadership, either from the lofty heights or from the isolated inner tent, did not inspire others to live above the petty squabbles which arise in congregational life.

The Lord is in love with people. God loves each of us as an only child. We meet the Divine most tenderly as secluded vessels of God's special interest. It is then God's Voice, God's Touch, and God's Presence comes to us and, thus, through us out to others.

As Jesus demonstrated so well, the desert is not a place in which one stays, it is a place to pass through and re-center for service to the Kingdom. It is from this *"new centeredness"* that we may use the strength and wisdom acquired in our desert experience to benefit those entrusted to our care.

The Bible uses the terms desert, wilderness, and lonely places interchangeably. The desert is a place beyond our control. Usually, we are resistant. Sometimes we are called to it; sometimes we are led to it. Sometimes life just dumps us there, whether we want to go or not.

Some insist the desert is a threatening evil. But why would Jesus hide away in such a foreboding place over and over? In the desert, we find ourselves terribly vulnerable. Alone.

Albeit, the Bible is replete with desert dwellers. It seems that the painful purification causes the itinerate nomad to depend whole-heartedly on God, thus coming out on the other side with blessed transformation, a gift to all.

Hear the descriptive depiction of the forerunner of Jesus, John the Baptist. *"So the child grew and became strong in spirit, and was in the deserts till the day of his manifestation to Israel."* Maybe that's it! Somehow, in the midst of our wilderness wanderings, our radical dependence on the Divine makes us humbly stout. *"When we are weak, then He is strong."*

Jesus and His cousin follow in the steps of the many of God's chosen. Abraham, at God's request, departed a thriving and affluent

Shhh...Listening For God

urban life to go out into the desert, not even knowing the way, but trusting that God would reveal a plan.

Likewise, Moses escaped into the desert of solitary contemplation for 60 years. Here he met the *ultra-pyromanian* at the *"burning bush,"* the God of the Hebrews, and was sent to tell of his encounter. In time, Israel herself wandered the desert for 40 years, and she will again be guarded there at the end of the age according to John the Revelator.

The desert is a theme of Jeremiah and other authors of the sandy scene. Elijah the prophet was called to leave the city of Tishbe in Gilead, and go into the desert. God not only provided for him, but also protected him from Jezebel and, in the process, taught him to hear the Voice of the Lord: . . .*but the LORD was not in the strong wind, but the LORD was not in the great earthquake, but the LORD was not in the ferocious fire. He spoke in a "still small voice."*

We need the desert. Jesus discovered this silent sustaining secret. Bishop of Lyons, Eucherius, summarizes the mastery:

> And the new Adam drove off the seducer of the old Adam. What a triumph for the desert, that the devil who was victorious in paradise should be vanquished in a wasteland.

We naturally think that a desert experience is something for the ill-behaved or the hard-headed. Jesus surely didn't qualify as either. Yet, it is in the desert He defeated the carnal-self provoked by the threat of evil, tempted with power.

In this story, after fasting for forty days, the Devil said to Jesus, *"Turn this stone into bread; worship me and all is thine; jump from*

148

this great height and the angels will catch thee. . ." Absolute power, they say, does corrupt absolutely. This was a necessary defeat. There is true power in meekness and humility.

As in wartime, Jesus strategically picked the terrain of battle. With only God and the Holy Spirit as His support, the desert experience fortified His resolve. There was nowhere else to go. There was no one else to call upon.

At some point in time, those who press into God's will, in all likelihood, pass through a similar experience. And I add, alone. Such trials are necessary; surely they draw us ever closer to our Divine connection. Our strength is found only in God's Power and Presence. Apart from God's Spirit we can do nothing.

Planning for our desert excursion, is not necessary, it will just come. The key is how we react when it gets here. We can resist it, or we can stretch out and breathe deeply to find God in the midst of the darkness. If we dismiss it we could miss the Divine plan of deepening our spiritual relationship.

Quoting biblical promises over the top of these uncomfortable feelings will not drive them away. When such sensations come, be careful, especially at the beginning. It is in the beginning when we may decide too hastily to suppress the troubling feelings of the soul. Press into these things. God may be at work. Look at it as God's Presence disrupting what is. The holy and the horrible are difficult to distinguish.

Shhh...Listening For God

Jesus discovered something healthy about seclusion with the purpose of meeting God and being touched by the Spirit. So, prayerfully give into the gnawing. When things are not as clear as desired, there is a tendency to peer through the dimness more fervently searching for the brightened path of God's direction. We must trust. Here we find rest, comfort, and real strength.

Isn't that the point? We learn most about God and self in the seasons of sufferings and trials.

Ever hear of the expression *The Dark Night of the Soul?* Besides being the title of numerous books, it is also a description of the lives of many people who have experienced a kind of illuminating darkness. Comtemplatives and mystics have used this language throughout Christian history to describe a period of their lives when they felt distanced from God. Reasons vary.

Gerald May, M.D., a practitioner of medicine and psychiatry, has written from a professional perspective a most informative piece analyzing the discussions between Teresa of Avila and Saint John of the Cross. Not everything negative that is going on in our lives can be attributed to a *"Dark Night"* experience.

According to the good doctor, a *Dark Night* does not necessarily reflect a bad period of illness, evil, or mere discouragement. Most accurately, *"Dark Night"* is a term that simply means *"obscure."*

We all have passed through extended times when the direction of our spiritual lives was fuzzy and God's Voice faint. Welcome to the

Dark Night of the Soul. Gerald May clarifies his understanding of what *"obscurity"* means in the lives of John and Teresa. Let's listen in:

> John's explanation of obscurity goes further. He says that in worldly matters it is good to have light so we know where to go without stumbling. But in spiritual matters it is precisely when we *do* think we know where to go that we are most likely to stumble. Thus, John says, God darkens our awareness *in order to keep us safe*. When we cannot chart our own course, we become vulnerable to God's protection, and the darkness becomes a "guiding night," a "night more kindly than the dawn."

In my own journey of pain and obscurity, I felt directed by the Lord to revisit the great song of protection, Psalm 91. *"He who dwelleth in the secret place of the most High. . ."* I had read this encouraging and hopeful Psalm many, many times to myself and to others, but didn't catch that *"dwelleth"* literally means *"to pass the night."*

Before my own personal walk in the unknown, my *Dark Night* rhetoric had always come from the accounts of those who had written of their own experiences, and not from an introspective analysis of the Psalmistic reference.

Upon studying this Psalm, I discovered with enlightened eyes that Scripture has its own comforting understanding of the *passing of the night*. And here, surprisingly, it unfolds in a journey through the Divine Names:

> He who dwelleth in the secret place of the most High [*El Elyon*] shall abide under the shadow of the Almighty [*Shaddai*]. I will say of the LORD [*Jehovah*], He is my refuge and my fortress; my God [*Elohim*]; in Him will I trust.

Shhh...Listening For God

The sequence of the Divine Names above appears in reverse of its chronological depiction in the Torah, especially through God's dealings with Abraham, the father of the Faith. Nevertheless, the author of the Psalm intentionally designates *El Elyon*, the most High, our crowning glory, the very outworking of our journey as we *"pass the night away."*

You can well imagine that each Divine Name has a specific revelatory impact on a surrendered life. For example, Abraham who followed in blind trust a path which was *obscure*. It was a walk of faith.

Let me briefly note that the Almighty, the *El Shaddai*, the One who pours in, desires empty vessels. We must be wanting and needing more. God promises to bless so that we can be a blessing. Thus the term *Shaddai* is most significant. As it was with Abraham, so it was with Job. In fact, the name *Shaddai* shows up more often in this ancient story than anywhere else in the Older Testament.

The countless questions of situation surrounding Job's life depleted him of *self-full-ness* and brought him into a position of complete and total emptiness. Only now can the Almighty's dramatic action of *"pouring forth"* be served. In the end, Job acquired twice as much as when he was living in full stride, at full speed.

Faith didn't attract God or move the Divine to fill Job's life with blessings which runneth over. It was emptiness. Ditto for Abraham. God patiently waits for the most opportune time, that moment when

Shhh...Listening For God

self runs dry. *Welcome to wherever you are.* When you are down and sometimes out, *look up, for your redemption draweth nigh.*

Job's desperate and admitted need, his hunger and thirst, was the catalyst that moved the Hand of the Almighty. In the end, Job's heart was softened and his generosity enhanced. For Job, life was now slower, but significantly more meaningful.

Coming through the struggles of a disruptive world, we can meekly embody the definitive purpose of our spiritual journey—to be wounded healers conformed into the image of Christ, priests of the most High God. Those who have learned to trust the unknown, even the darkness, have found it all to be a source of Divine connectivity.

Saint Paul wrote in the Newer Testament to the Church of Corinth. In The Message Bible by Eugene Peterson this section is titled, *The Rescue. "All praise to the God and Father of our Master, Jesus the Messiah! Father of all Mercy! God of all healing counsel! He comes alongside us when we go through hard times, and before you know it, He brings us alongside someone else who is going through hard times so that we can be there for that person just as God was there for us."* How priestly. How Christlike.

Jesus always returned empowered from His *"Dark Nights"* in the wilderness. And now we know how and why. **Emptiness attracts fullness. Retreat fuels advance.** Jesus said, *"The Son can do nothing of Himself, but what He sees the Father do."* Where did Jesus go to *"see?"* Solitude. Where did Jesus go to *"hear?"* Silence.

Shhh...Listening For God

Jesus' empowerment of the Spirit was demonstrated by His proclamations, His willingness, and His ability to help others in need with the power of the Holy Spirit. He was blessed to be a blessing.

Shall we follow in His ways? The formula is simple: separate, sanctify, search, supplicate, and see.

Shhh...Listening For God

Listening for God Discussion Questions
Chapter 9 – Quiet Places, Sacred Spaces

1. Jesus chose to go into the wilderness of solitude. Where can you go to do the same?

2. Why do you think solitude frightens us?

3. Desert experiences can be life changing. What happened to you?

4. Have you experienced transformation that results from a desert wandering? Where you led there, taken there or just dumped there?

5. What are some instances where you have experienced spiritual dryness?

Chapter Ten

A VOICE IN THE WILDERNESS

Nestled in the rolling countryside just outside of Jerusalem is a quaint little village, *Ein Karem,* the birthplace of John the Baptist. I have strolled along the picturesque lanes several times enjoying a little shopping and a memorable lunch or two with friends.

It is easy to imagine John as a small lad playing boyhood games like the many children who still criss-cross the streets with excitement.

Pilgrims fill their souvenir plastic bottles from Mary's Well while ignoring the printed signs in several languages, *"Do Not Drink the Water."* In this hometown of Elizabeth, local inhabitants, no doubt, have drawn water from these same springs for centuries.

Steep, rocky slopes support the Christian shrines that commemorate special biblical events like Mary's song, *The Magnificat,* the response to her cousin Elizabeth's declaration regarding the forthcoming birth of the Christ.

> My soul magnifies the Lord, and my spirit has rejoiced in God my Savior. For He has regarded the lowly state of His maidservant; for behold, henceforth all generations will call me blessed.

157

Shhh...Listening For God

Shortly after the Angelic visitation by Gabriel in Nazareth, Mary, in hasty fashion, came to *Ein Karem*, one hundred miles south in the hill country of Judea. She stayed with Zacharias and Elizabeth for three months.

As the story goes, Elizabeth, of the daughters of Aaron, was well advanced in years and barren. Elizabeth's husband, Zacharias, was performing his duties as a priest less than a day's walk from Jerusalem. Both husband and wife were considered righteous before God.

In those days, to be barren was a disgrace. Conversely, to give birth, especially to a son, fostered the family lineage and was thus perceived as a blessing directly from the LORD. Elizabeth's barrenness likely contributed to as many rumors as Mary's forthcoming miraculous virgin pregnancy.

There is little doubt that both Mary and Elizabeth endured the usual tongue wagging of small-town hearsay. It's sad to think that people haven't changed much after all these years. **Gossip prevails even among the reborn; the notorious grapevine needs our shears, not our ears.**

God surely selects unlikely characters to reveal Divine plans. God is not afraid of scandal. While neighbors appear blind and resistant to the supernatural elements in play, Heaven employs Angels.

Where would we be without Angels? Several times I have felt their protective intervention, a slight nudge here and there, guiding my sliding automobile past a dangerous intersection promising disaster and death. Besides, how many other unknown encounters

Shhh...Listening For God

have I experienced unaware of their cloaked appearance? Only God and the Angels know for sure.

Without Angels, the biblical narrative would be stripped of its essence. Humankind remains in need of their pronouncements and involvement. In the Christmas story they abound.

While standing in the Temple on the right side of the Altar of Incense, for example, an Angel appeared to Zacharias. In a holy prayerful act, he offered to God the sweet smelling incense representing the worship of the people.

As flower children of the psychedelic years, we burned incense all the time. We used the furry-feelin' perfumed sticks to hide the scent of our sins from others. The distinct aroma of dried leaves, and anything else smoked, that might help us to escape our vacant lives in favor of a trip into *another time and another place.*

Incense burned in Scripture is typically thought of as our prayers rising up before God. For instance, in the book of Revelation, John writes by the Spirit of inspiration, *"And the smoke of the incense, with the prayers of the saints, ascended before God from the angel's hand."*

The Gospel writer, Luke the physician, describes the upward smoke as an answer coming down:

But the angel said to him, "Do not be afraid, Zacharias, for your prayer is heard; and your wife Elizabeth will bear you a son, and you shall call his name John. . ."

"He will also be filled with the Holy Spirit, even from his mother's womb. And he will turn many of the children of Israel to the Lord their God."

Shhh...Listening For God

In 1999 the first archaeological evidence of John the Baptist emerged. A cave was discovered in the orchards of a kibbutz near *Ein Karem*. Byzantine monks used the cave as a Christian holy place in the fourth and fifth centuries. On the walls are drawings telling the life story of this leather clad *"honey and locust"* eating stranger. Having been there, I can testify it is quite astounding.

Inside the entrance there is an unusual foot-anointing stone in which a baptismal candidate could place his or her foot neatly into the etched shape, as I did. This ancient water reservoir and first century *Mikvah* (ritual cleansing pool) is believed to be the place where John first sought solitude in the wilderness.

Not only is John's birth unique, but the place and purpose of his ministry are also remarkable. Whenever people are called to be used of God, they are more than likely to find the themselves wandering in the wilderness, like the many faithful before them.

Paul of Tarsus, a man well educated, spent three years in solitude in the Sinai of Arabia. Matthew Easton called this time of mysterious separation a *"breathless calm which ushers in the tumultuous storm of his active missionary life."*

Was Paul surrendering all his earthly knowledge in exchange for the Heavenly? *"Tarsus"* indicated locality as well as the educational pedigree of this so called humble *"tentmaker."* It is equivalent to something like Ph.D. Seemingly, God enhanced Paul's powers of reason and used them to write most of what is considered the New

Shhh...Listening For God

Testament today. The old quip is true: *A book will travel to places and peoples the author will never see.*

Are solitude and silence that significant? It is difficult to ignore the repeated theme of the wilderness in the lives of those who wish to walk with the Divine. At the end of his life, Serbian hermit, Father Arsenius said, *"I have often repented of having spoken, but never of having kept silent."*

Only in the wilderness of solitude do we look into the mirror of self and witness our reflection. Alone with nowhere else to go, quiet with no one else to engage, we ever so cautiously move within and meet the stark, naked truth of self. Louis Bouyer reveals:

Solitude is a terrible trial, for it serves to crack open and burst apart the shell of our superficial securities. It opens out to us the unknown abyss that we all carry within us. . .[and] discloses the fact that these abysses are haunted.

This wading into the deep occurs certainly and unerringly through the restorative caressing of the Hand of the Great Physician.

The voice that arises out of such solitude is the voice of authority. Jesus was praised and challenged for such qualities: *". . .the people were astonished at His doctrine; for He taught them as one having authority, and not as the scribes."* This is to be expected. **One who comes with depth of freedom in his or her words need not use enforced volume or radical intonations. Listeners know when such people have been with God. The speaker is assured as well.**

Shhh...Listening For God

Authoritative voice comes when the surrendered have been empowered by something other than learned skill and repeated oration. Their eyes have been opened. Their tongues have been loosed. Their ears have heard of that for which we all long. Our role is but to sit, listen, and follow the well trodden path to enlightenment.

Zacharias dismissed Gabriel's authoritative voice and suffered the consequence.

> And Zacharias said to the angel, "How shall I know this? For I am an old man, and my wife is well advanced in years."
>
> And the angel answered and said to him, "I am Gabriel, who stands in the presence of God, and was sent to speak to you and bring you these glad tidings. But behold, you will be mute and not able to speak until the day these things take place, because you did not believe my words which will be fulfilled in their own time."

After nine months of imposed muteness, Zacharias emerged with new vistas. It was common, if not expected, to name a child after the father. But solitude and silence had completed their inner work and caused him to hear and know from a different perspective. No longer following the crowd, doing what was expected, Zacharias did the scandalous. He named his son "*John.*"

It was silence that permitted Zacharias to understand finally the specific role of his son as a forerunner. It was silence that allowed Zacharias to discern the Divine role of Mary and the Incarnate One who was to be born in just a few short months.

The New Testament begins like the Old. Silence, then voice.

162

Shhh...Listening For God

Listening, then proclamation. Void, then a new created order.

Words that flow forth from a marked period of retreat are most penetratingly powerful. More consecutively spoken words are attributed to Zacharias than any other character in the Gospel accounts except Jesus. The silence of Zacharias was what made the plan of God so powerfully heard. In fact, among the many expressions of honorific praise which fell from the lips of this dutiful priest was the famous prayer, *The Benedictus*.

In the Church's Liturgy of the Hours, Zacharias' humble homage is included each day in the Morning Prayers (formerly Lauds) which have issued forth for untold years.

> "Blessed *is* the Lord God of Israel, for He has visited and redeemed His people, and has raised up a horn of salvation for us in the house of His servant David, as He spoke by the mouth of His holy prophets, who *have been* since the world began, that we should be saved from our enemies and from the hand of all who hate us, to perform the mercy *promised* to our fathers and to remember His holy covenant, the oath which He swore to our father Abraham: to grant us that we, being delivered from the hand of our enemies, might serve Him without fear, in holiness and righteousness before Him all the days of our life."

> "And you, child, will be called the prophet of the Highest; for you will go before the face of the Lord to prepare His ways, to give knowledge of salvation to His people by the remission of their sins, through the tender mercy of our God, with which the Dayspring from on high has visited us; to give light to those who sit in darkness and the shadow of death, to guide our feet into the way of peace."
>
> Luke 1:68-79

Shhh...Listening For God

Morning Prayer is that period of day that takes us out of darkness and into the light. At sunrise, we receive the new day as a gift, the gift of opportunity. Our attitudes, endeavors, and hopes thereupon are turned with expectancy.

I read a story of a man whose jaw was wired shut for many months. At the grand opening, he answered inquiries as to what it was like not being able to speak for so long. His response? *"I never learned so much."* Listening, true listening, is the outcome of true silence.

History records many instances when a voice was needed and no one was ready. Or, a voice was sounding and no one was listening. Reading an article *"The Sound of Silence"* triggered my historic interests. Why was it that the world remained shamefully quiet when the persecution of the Jews began pre WWII? Silence is meant to empower, not impede.

In 1935, the Nuremberg Laws relegated the Jews to second-class citizenship, setting the stage for what was about to come. Signs in windows were posted much like discriminatory statements against Negro civilians in the United States: *"Jews Enter At Your Own Risk."* Only the race and place had changed. Prejudice—the product of a poisoned mind and heart—continues to wield its ugly head.

November 9, 1935 will ever be remembered as *"The Night of Broken Glass."* Germans of every age, class, and gender joined the brutalities without any provocation or encouragement from the Nazi hierarchy. Windows of Jewish establishments and businesses as well as Synagogues and homes were smashed. Streets were littered

Shhh...Listening For God

with sharply edged shattered pieces estimated in value by an insurance expert to be 6 million dollars for non-Jewish landlords alone, an astonishing sum in the 1930s.

How could the sound of breaking glass not be heard? Remarkably, informed nations of the world watched with a seeming tolerance. The following morning, German citizens casually observed as Jews were carted off to restricted locations, literally escorted to their deaths.

But now these violent public actions could no longer be hidden away. They brought to the attention of the global community three concentration camps, including the infamous *Dachau*. Still no one spoke. No one challenged or questioned or inquired. Genocide had begun. *Holocaust*.

It has been said we can *"sit out"* only one *Holocaust* in a lifetime. Undoubtedly, one is too many. If you were born after 1973 then you are a survivor of the holocaust of abortion. One-third of this generation did not survive. Count yourself and your family blessed to be alive.

I have had opportunity to watch old films from the Civil Rights Era. I've seen how African Americans, marching in non-violent protest were mistreated. They were beaten with clubs, bitten by dogs, knocked down with fire hoses for simply walking from here to there in a small southern town called Selma.

Where was I? Did I speak up against injustice? No, forgive me, I didn't. My head was in the *"clouds,"* a smokey fog of unrealistic

Shhh...Listening For God

anticipations that somehow thought in total naïveté we will just all get along. Where were you?

I walked for peace, but it never came. It only comes when we pray for it, and pray ardently. And then seek to uphold it *"with liberty and justice for ALL!"*

How do you feel about genocide? What about Iraq? Rwanda? Libya? Where next?

The salutation by Jesus in the Upper Room, *"Peace be unto you,"* is the greeting of a new life in Christ that spreads out to a world in tragic disruption. Almost every document in the New Testament written after the Gospels begins with the same greeting, "Peace." Peace with God. Peace with self. Peace with others.

Thus it is here, in the turmoil of life, that we come closest to understanding what it means to *work out our own salvation with fear and trembling.* For those who dare practice the spiritual disciplines of simplicity, silence, and solitude. . .beware. It comes with a certain responsibility.

Yes, we will meet God. We will feel God's Touch like never before. We will be close to the Divine Spirit, ever so close. But God will whisper. God will tell us of the injustices of the aborted, the poor, the uprooted, the abandoned, the wounded, the broken, and the abused.

Can we sit idly in God's Presence merely soaking in bountiful goodness and gracious kindness? No. We will be sent.

Shhh...Listening For God

The pilgrimage into silence comes with a cost. Certainly, there are things we must give up in order to quiet self and setting. **But if we want to go further, or as some prefer to say, deeper, solitude and silence greet us as awaiting doormen and usher us into the enigma of the supernatural, that which is beyond what we see with our eyes and feel with our hands.**

Entering the realm of the Spirit, a fuller life in God is really what we are after. Few seem to want to pay the price. Spiritual is not magical. Enlightenment does not come effortlessly.

During the Samaritan Revival in the book of Acts, glorious things took place: exorcisms, miracles, healings, conversions, *"and there was great joy in that city."* A sorcerer named Simon also came to the Lord in that mighty demonstration of God's Spirit. Simon confessed Christ, yet something was still amiss in his bewitching soul.

Simon wanted to purchase with money what he saw the Apostles doing so that he could manifest similar power through the laying on of his hands (Acts 8). Seen any TV preachers lately? Many seem not all that dissimilar from our context thinking blessings can be acquired by eliciting donations. Peter was forthright: *"Simon. . .your heart is not right in the sight of God."*

Conversion is a beginning, a clearing away of the debris which had prohibited us from hearing the Gospel of Christ. This clearing away isn't easy. Minds must be renewed and hearts must be guarded. Though they die hard, old habits must be replaced. We must protect the heart at all costs, for in the words of the proverbial writer *"Keep your heart with all diligence, for out of it spring the issues of life."*

Three years after his surgery, a heart transplant recipient and his mother were almost thirty minutes overdue for a meeting in the hospital chapel with the wife of the donor. Such meetings are rare. Being a half-hour late created suspicions for those involved that perhaps this was not a good idea after all.

The physician coordinating the meeting had just recommended cancelling the gathering. Then, the wife of the donor spoke up. *"No, we have to wait. He's here in the hospital. I felt him arrive thirty minutes ago. I felt my husband's presence. Please wait with me."*

No sooner had she spoken and the two entered the room. They had arrived at the hospital thirty minutes earlier, but had trouble finding the designated space, the chapel. The doctor was now seriously intrigued.

The young man who received a new heart was using new words, significant words, known only heretofore by the donor. He also listened to the donor's favorite type of music. He was now eating different foods, the favorite foods of the one who had so graciously donated his heart so that another could live.

Fascinating isn't it. How could the woman discern that the heart of her deceased husband had entered the building at a precise moment? How could the heart recipient know the donor's specific vocabulary and preferred edibles? Authors of the *Living Energy Universe* address this in their treatment of the human heart and how its memory and intelligence lie outside the brain's control. Dr. Schwartz and Dr. Russek muse:

> Our electromagnetic signals always precede us. Some physicists go so far as to propose that personal information actually "travels" instantaneously. . .while the body, obliviously, lags way behind at a snail's pace.

In light of this organ transplant of living memory, loving God with all *"our heart"* takes on new significance. We need a cardio makeover. And this Inward Journey is a paramount must.

My good friend, Dr. Mahoney, routinely shares how people carry their painful distresses with them wherever they go. Could it be that the attitudes and emotions of others enter our personal space before the individual even arrives? Does this explain why preaching in certain places is sometimes so hard? After all, who knows what kinds of despair have seeped into what we call *"Sanctuary"* each and every Sunday.

Time for a check up, and not from the neck up, but from the neck down. Jesus taught us much evil proceeds from the heart: obscenities, greed, depravity, deceptive dealings, carousing, mean looks, slander, arrogance, foolishness— *"all these are vomit from the heart."*

Ever have to clean-up vomit? Not an easy task. It takes time, gloves, bleach, rags, something to hold your nose closed. Try pinching it between two fingers from one hand while cleaning with the other. The imagery is rather strong, but so is the seriousness of

Shhh...Listening For God

Jesus' observation. The old adage rings true that *an ounce of prevention is worth a pound of cure*.

The practice of solitude and silence is the process whereby we are *"strengthened with might by His Spirit in the inner man."* In my many decades of Christian experience, I have been exposed to countless doctrinal fads and so called experiential solutions. Nothing, however, replaces the practices of Jesus and of the Prophets before Him, and of the multitude of Saints since then.

Solitude and silence are always in the picture when there is true renewal. Without them, we simply play on the peripheral threshold, enjoyable yes, and spiritual at times. But we never quite enter the depth of the Spirit that is available to us.

We say we are *"Led by the Spirit,"* but are we? We seem to be still a fair distance away from what is portrayed in the pages of the Bible. We want more or we wouldn't have come this far. But are we ready?

Our adventure into the life of the Spirit begins with desire. From desire we can begin to pray for the sanctification of our soul. We dedicate our thoughts to God.

Hear the heart. It longs for that of which I speak. Follow these longings. They are promptings of the Spirit. *"How,"* you say? Solitude. Separate yourself from the crowds, the hurry, and the noise. Meet with God. *"How,"* you say? Through the silence of listening. Ask the LORD to meet you, say *"Come, Holy Spirit,"* then listen.

Shhh...Listening For God

God's Voice is soft and clear, filled with hope and always reassuring. Listen within, deep within. The Spirit speaks of God's great love for you. *Shhh. . .* Did you hear that?

Listening for God Discussion Questions
Chapter 10 – A Voice in the Wilderness

1. When have you been protected by the angels? Did you give God the credit?

2. Have you ever wished you had spoken up instead of keeping silent? What were the circumstances and why do you regret keeping quiet?

3. Have you spent a time in the wilderness of solitude? Did you feel empowered afterward? Did you feel you were *"sent"* or directed to take a specific action?

4. Does your heart long for more leading of the Holy Spirit?

Chapter Eleven

A WORD FROM THE LORD

If I said I was hearing voices, you might become a little worried about my mental and emotional state. *"Working too hard again?" "Are you getting enough rest?" "Have you seen a Mental Health Specialist?"* Typical responses to anyone who might disclose such inward discussions. *"Just exactly how many voices are you hearing in there pastor?"*

It all sounds somewhat reminiscent of a scene right out of Ghostbusters or more graphically, The Exorcism of Emily Rose.

"I talk with God" raises an eyebrow or two most anywhere. After all, many conclude such things to be myths, or the primitive thinking of a time long, long ago. Possibly a story or a song will focus us more particularly: *Who's afraid of the big bad wolf? The big bad wolf, the big bad, wolf?* Who? Me!!!

Dr. Max Case says we need *"Third Pig Thinking."* The other two pigs in our treasured childhood lore viewed life with a playful attitude causing them to be unprepared for attacks from their prowling white-fanged enemy. He was big and ferocious and could blow down any house made of straw or sticks.

"Third Pig Thinking" means to develop a befitting strategy against the relentless enemy of our souls. It requires a paradigm shift. Instead of being victims of the forces of life, we must exert God-ordained authority over these hostile coercions.

Listening for God is a paradigmatic approach. Intentional listening positions us as responsible owners of our own dwellings. Since God talks and God cares, God will guide, even *"warning us of things to come."* God strengthens us to withstand the winds of destruction intended for our soulistic downfalls.

Listening for God is a deliberate act. Listening was the initial posture of creation and creature. Listening was the principle purpose in the architectural design of the Temple. Throughout Scripture, listening was the main role of the Prophets, Rulers, Judges, and Priests.

So what's up? George Barna, research analyst, notes, *"Americans believe in God and think religion is important, but they want to make their own rules."* It is no secret, we must come to the Throne on God's terms, not ours. Nothing too difficult. As Micah the Prophet records, *"He has shewed thee, O man, what is good; and what doth the LORD require of thee, but to do justly, and to love mercy, and to walk humbly with thy God."*

This famed trilogy has been a helpful filter by which all my thoughts, all my actions, and all my decisions must pass. It changes everything for me and those with whom I journey.

Shhh...Listening For God

On one of my early trips to the Holy Land, I had a Jewish guide, Elle, who doubled all his verbiage. *"Hello, hello,"* he would answer the phone. *"Quickly, quickly,"* as he hurried us through an archaeological wonder. I often laughed that Elle may have developed his unique duplication from Jesus' *"Verily, verily."*

Seriously, in tender moments of historic importance, Elle would lower his voice and ever so softly mutter with a phlegm-filled hoarseness, *"Slowly, slowly."* I have followed that mantra for decades.

For the workaholic who lives in high gear, *"Slowly, slowly"* helps me soften my hectic ways into a more God honoring flow. *"Slowly"* is very, very important. No matter how many times I read the story of the Big Race, the tortoise always wins.

As a result, I have lowered my blood pressure significantly and, hopefully, have become less demanding of those around me. I am here to enjoy the journey and the many I meet along the way. Hello friend.

In this hectic, fast-paced world there is a hurried attempt to hear God on the run. The prayer closet has categorically morphed and is now the front seat of an automobile. Prayer is rushed as we drive to and from work, inviting God in at stop signs, intersections, and traffic jams. On the positive side, this *"prayer"* may cut down on the number of expressive hand gestures. Prayer postures prepare us for an encounter with the Divine Presence whether we kneel, sit, stand, or lay.

What is difficult for most of God's children is that we have not learned to recognize God's Voice. We are missing spiritual intentionality. Among the myriad of messages passing through us, we are trying to distinguish Divine Voice from our own, our own voice from well meaning friends, and the voices of friends from others and God. I often find myself exhausted before I even start, if not totally confused.

To implement quietness into our devotional lives is a bit risky. The only real thing we know about silence is likely negative. Solitary confinement is a sentence imposed for bad behavior. Silence in a relationship means problems, maybe suppressed anger on the verge of boiling over into unwanted violence.

Theologically, we have language to describe God, to discuss God, and to define God, but somewhere along the way we have lost the simplicity of just being with God. God does not operate solely in the realm of the spectacular.

Pentecostals, Charismatics, and/or Third Wave believers may exhibit an imbalance in this area. In our churches there is a flurry of activity and plenty of jubilance, while ignoring the still and the quiet. If, by chance, a Holy Hush should descend, we can be sure it will be interrupted by a well-meaning prophetic proclaimer or personal testimony. Church announcements break the serene. Stillness makes us nervous. We use words to cover our fear.

Silence and solitude help preserve Christian practice from fanaticism as much as praise and giftings help preserve it from stale routines. As posted sentries, solitude and silence keep in check our delusions of power, zeal, and pride, a constant challenge. Only in silence do we realize how truly empty and fractured we really are. Each of us, as Christian brothers and sisters, must grasp the apparent—our strength comes from the Lord.

"Why aren't more people used by God?" is a question I am often asked. It is not that we are too weak, rather we are too strong, so strong we cannot with any true humility strike our breast. *"To come boldly"* means to come with freedom of speech, to freely talk with the Divine, not brashly demand. We are not used because we are not free. In fact, we are enslaved.

What will it take to move our vehicles into the slow lane? A ticking in the engine? A thumping in the tire? Smoke from under the hood? How about a pain in the neck? A chest pain here, an ulcer there, failed marriage, rowdy children, or an arrest might do it? Why wait for a catastrophe or a trial of nerves? I'm not sure why we procrastinate until the Doctor says, *"Slow down or else."* Hey, I'm a Doctor.

Silence is a biblical model. Solitude is a spiritual principle. Throughout each day, we should experience these tender moments, but often we do not stay long enough for all the visitors to leave. Our minds race, thoughts run, voices call. Nouwen shares his own struggle: *"The task is to persevere in my solitude, to stay in my cell until all my seductive visitors get tired of pounding on my door and leave me alone."* Wait, oh just a little bit longer. A fresh word goes a long way in getting on with life. It's in silence and solitude that the freedom comes.

Shhh...Listening For God

There is within each of us a desperate need to arrive at a point where we can distinguish God's oral communiqué from all other human banter, a Voice clear, familiar, and significant. So, how do we arrive at such a maturation?

When Glen Clark interviewed renowned black scientist, George Washington Carver, he asked what was the key to his success in discovering so many of the secrets of nature. Carver replied, *". . .all my life I have risen at four o'clock and have gone into the woods and talked with God and listened for His 'Voice.' There God gives me my orders for the day. . .when people are still asleep I hear God best and learn my plan."*

Immersing ourselves in locales where God has provided us opportunity to hear is a great way to start. And I mean, the use of prayer, a special place for prayer, and designated prayer time will nurture our spiritual development.

In the Book of books, there is a descriptive interchange in which God spoke audibly to Jesus. It is worthy of note that Jesus is the only individual who heard and discerned the message. Why? Out of all who were present, Jesus was the only One who had nurtured an intimate relationship with Creator God. How? Silence, solitude, and simplicity (SSS). This SSS works rather well. If it was good enough for Jesus, it will be good enough for us and anyone else willing to proceed into the Glory.

Can we be assured Scripturally that we can expect to hear a the Divine Voice? Let's review the matter. In the Gospels, God spoke

Shhh...Listening For God

audibly to Jesus on three occasions: at the beginning of His ministry (baptism), at the turning point of His ministry (transfiguration) and near the culmination of His ministry (obedience). Jesus says:

> Now is My soul troubled; and what shall I say? Father, save Me from this hour: but for this cause came I unto this hour. Father, glorify Thy Name. Then came there a Voice from Heaven, saying, I have both glorified it, and will glorify it again. The people therefore, that stood by, and heard it, said that it thundered: others said, An Angel spake to Him. Jesus answered and said, This Voice came not because of Me, but for your sakes.
>
> John 12:27-30

The beloved Apostle John paints a portrait of Jesus' prayerful struggle in the Garden of Gethsemane between questioning God and trusting God, doubting God and believing God. Let me suggest this scenario. *If it is possible take this cup from Me. No, this cup of suffering is why I have come. I will sacrificially die so that others might live.* Scarlet droplets stream down His face, revealing the tension between the two realms. God will reassure any of us who face such life challenges.

John shows us a threefold reaction of those who walked with Jesus. Every crowd is somewhat mixed. Each Sunday morning is not much different.

There are always the naysayers. Of course, there are the faithful few. And there are those who just gather out of snoopery. The latter think to themselves, perhaps this God does exist and might just do or say something significant this very day.

179

Shhh...Listening For God

In our selected passage, skeptics were present. Skeptics usually offer a hypothesis never requested, a natural explanation of a supernatural cause. The curious admit something extraordinary happened and are impressed by the demonstration; however, they did not understand what the Voice said. Something similar happened on the road to Damascus to Saul's companions as they traveled the transformational path with their friend soon to be called Paul.

As noted above, believing followers were also gathered with Jesus. These are those who affirmed that God spoke and Divine amplifications could be clearly discerned and understood.

Jesus gives us important clarity. This Voice was *"not for My Sake, but for your sakes."* If the crowd was somehow definitively prevented from earthly perception, why would Jesus say *"it was for you?"* No, Jesus teaches implicitly: God spoke and still speaks, although our spiritual attitudes and disposition either help or hinder the hearing of what God is saying.

By the time Jesus visited Jerusalem, the leaders and the people had accepted a Rabbinical notion that God had ceased to speak directly to them. A Hebraic expression, *Bath qol,* meant the *"Daughter of a voice,"* an echo, a faint whisper instead of straightforward communication from God. Accordingly, the time period between the Testaments is rather quiet.

The person of Jesus demonstrates that at major crossroads in life, we should anticipate to hear from the Heavenly Abode. **In difficult times, it is time to get quiet.** Irish writer, Samuel Becket said, *"Every* *word is an unnecessary stain on silence and nothingness."* Perhaps we have talked too much. *"Quietly, quietly."*

A word from the LORD spoken to a listening soul fortifies that life with encouragement, knowledge, and strength. As believers, we must live on the last clear word from Above, until we receive another. In between those moments, Scripture becomes our underpinning, teaching us and sustaining us on the journey

Voice comes from a beautiful Greek word *phone.* And this *Voice* is for us. It is not a faint tone, or a mere echo of what somebody else has already said. It engages and shapes us. *Phone* is an etymological root for the functionality of sound, as in phonograph or telephone.

In the Rock Era, a song written by Pete Seeger was recorded by an American band called *The Byrds.* Their style was distinguished by the use of a 12-string guitar and vocal harmony which melded the British Invasion sound with trace elements of folk and pop music. In 1991 they were inducted into the Rock 'n' Roll Hall of Fame in Cleveland, Ohio. They are listed as number 45 in the 100 greatest artists of all time.

Seeger's unforgettable melody and biblical poetry created the hit *"Turn, Turn, Turn."* His inspiration was drawn from the book of Ecclesiastes and takes the listener through a series of existential seasons, *"a time to every purpose under the Heaven."* For instance, there is *"A time to be born, and a time to die. . .A time to weep, and a time to laugh; a time to mourn, a time to dance."* These speak powerfully to our lives, of course.

But there is another prescribed balance. For a little later, the wise biblical lyricist also proclaimed, *"a time to keep silence, and a time to speak."* It is necessary that you and I insightfully know the difference.

Talkativeness is a disturbing characteristic. Much speech often makes one question the spiritual awareness of the *"talkateer."* It is funny how we can use a multiplicity of words to cover the shallowness of our souls.

People who talk a lot seem deaf to their verbal barrage. In an attempt to be the center of attention, the chatty continue in spite of the resistant reactions of those pulling away. Control of the tongue is a major factor in generating biblical wisdom.

When we step toward solitude and silence, our awareness of windy allocution is heightened. All of a sudden, our inner lives find wordiness a bit tedious. Our spirits are agitated, alarmed by the verbal onslaught which lacks meaning or insight. On this point, we may measure spiritual growth.

At one time, we probably blabbered on exactly like that which now irritates the monkish part of ourselves. But we have attached ourselves to a known and sure oath: *"be swift to hear, slow to speak, slow to wrath."*

Practicing slowness of speech solves a great deal of problems in life. Not only would we speak more slowly, our lives would also move more slowly. In so doing, we experience the *Shalom* of God.

Spending time with God allows the only One who truly cares about our personal well-being to properly shape it. A word of

Shhh...Listening For God

assurance from Above lasts us a long while, regardless of what others might declare at work or play the very next day. If God says it, then it must be true, and thus we believe it. It is in the practice of prayer that we are *"conformed"* as God wills.

Prayer time needs to be specific. Give God time to say to you those chosen words of comfort and edification. It might help for you to select a place of prayer that is comfortable and pleasant. It could be outdoors or indoors, like a special chair. Or use the gift of imagination. . .pick an image, a room, a cabin, that certain somewhere of memory where Jesus can meet with you alone, uninterrupted. Only you have the key. Only you know where.

Then invite Jesus in. He will meet with you there. When you sense His Presence, ask Him to tell you something. And in the quiet of your heart, He will.

Shhh...Listening For God

Listening for God Discussion Questions
Chapter 11 – A Word from the Lord

1. Do you expect to hear God when you are on the run?

2. Explain how you discern God's Voice among many?

3. Have you dealt with a life threatening challenge?

4. Are you troubled by noise and wordiness?

5. When does God's Voice seem clearest? Is it in seasons of suffering, in seasons of joy, or in everyday life?

Chapter Twelve

RUN SILENT, RUN DEEP

My father passed away as a young man by most standards, age 52, a day before my December birthday. I deeply miss his commanding presence, especially when life gets tough and I wonder if I can keep going.

Private First Class, Carl G. May, a man who loved sports and the outdoors, made frequent family fishing trips to the Great White North, a memory lane of Canadian adventure. Boyhood vacations were captivating combinations of camping and fishing, an environment which fostered responsible activity for the development of young lives. He would have dearly cherished my sons, Joel and Nathan. He died too soon.

In World War II, my dad was a paratrooper and saw limited action in India. I still review from time to time, the small 2 ½ x 3 ½ black and white photos he sent home from his stay abroad. After the war, like most GI's, he settled down, married, and started his family.

"Bud," as he was nicknamed, was a part-time police officer. He survived the global conflict only to be shot in the chest later in life

Shhh...Listening For God

in a domestic dispute. Identifying his naked body through a glass window with my two older brothers has etched an image far back in the recesses of my mostly blocked recollection. Like a stain on the wall, it bleeds through every now and then, requiring touch-up and another layer of fresh paint.

Whether our loved one is draped in a flag or wrapped in white linen, grief is the same. The folding of our nation's colors and a 21 gun salute ripple through my soul even now. Then those inspiring words, *"On behalf of the President of the United States. . ."*

I am beholden to my father for a number of things: discipline, work ethics, laughter and family, and dedication to a task. Even now I find strength in his memory. He was broad chested, muscularly defined, and a golden glove boxer. He and my Uncle Arnold, another feisty family character, cleared out a few taverns in their time.

Most distinctly, I recall one Monday morning as I readied myself to commute the twenty minutes from home for another day of college. Tensions had built on the Kent State University campus. The Ohio National Guard was standing watch with a camouflaged tank on the corner. Bomb scares were common at the time. Some days, all classes were cancelled.

On the 4th of May, my father uttered his provocative restriction, *"You're not going to school today. Somebody is going to get shot."* My life was surely spared by this rugged man who struggled between showing loving tenderness and unbending nerves of steel.

I am grateful for my father's forethought that somber day,

Shhh...Listening For God

because the bright blue and yellow school colors were soon to fly at half-staff. Crosby, Stills, Nash & Young sang the tragic anthem, *"Four Dead in O-hi-o."*

My dad never talked much about his experience in World War II, at least that I can remember. This is not unusual. I know many who have witnessed the horror of armed conflict and keep that door of their past tightly closed and bolted shut.

My father was an honorable veteran who courageously reared three young, blond haired hellions. Viewing scary movies through slotted fingers, like Ghoulardi (Ernie Anderson) on our local TV channel, was common in our household on late Friday nights.

Throughout the evening, Ghoulardi would poke innocent fun of local landmarks and known city personalities. We had our own *"Parmageist"* as he mocked the large silver-ball yard ornaments and assorted pink flamingos displayed on the lawns by the white-sock'd residents of our pierogi capital of Cleveland's Westside.

On other days, we sat in front of the tubed picture box mesmerized by the old war films such as *Pork Chop Hill* or the weekly television program, *Combat!* My father sporadically narrated.

Wartime classics brought to light the necessarily futile, and yet valiant, effort of dedicated men who fought for a piece of dirt, a lone hill in the middle of somewhere that was considered of strategic value. In time, no one seems to care about what was so highly contested. In war neither side really wins.

Shhh...Listening For God

But it is the tense 1958 naval film *Run Silent, Run Deep* that sticks in my mind. This dramatic story is about a submarine commander of the U.S.S. Nerka, P. J. Richardson. Captain Richardson was pursuing, with angered vengeance, a Japanese Battleship very much like Captain Ahab chased the white beast Moby Dick, which had torturously injured his body and mind in prior jousts.

The submerged vessel silently slithered through enemy waters looking and waiting for its ironclad target. Famous Hollywood names completed the blockbuster cast: Clark Gable, Burt Lancaster, and Don Rickles in his film debut.

Submarines are unique boats. Underwater they run in calm currents totally removed from the turbulence on the surface. In wartime, the enemy circles above in methodic pursuit. When the submarine is detected, depth charges slowly sink to explosive levels creating waves of destructive vibration and upward water spouts of release.

Meanwhile, the tubular container and its regimented crew are unthwarted by the perilous conditions. In defense, they have descended into safer waters, into deeper waters.

Submarines survive the enormous external pressure on their hull by compensating with equal pressure within. Cruising under the blustering waves associated with the squalls on the watery veneer, the ships remain safely indifferent to tidal storms, enemy presence, and the dark of night.

Run Silent, Run Deep, a submarine's stealth tactic, allows those properly trained to travel under the peering radar of any pursuer.

Survival, as well as victory, thus lies in the practice of the disciplines, the daily drills, going through the required motions over and over. To hesitate may put the captain and crew in mortal danger. Habits ensure safety in the time of crisis.

The religious implications are obvious. *Run Silent, Run Deep* is an excellent metaphor of the spiritual life. The greater the silence, the greater the depth of Spirit. The greater the Spirit, the greater the safety, and the clearer the guidance. This teaches us that the silence of monasticism is inherently reasonable. Silence is always a required precursor to more. Sister Hall observes:

> We are told that Mary pondered the word in the silence of her heart (Luke 2:51), and obviously the beloved disciple listened deeply, in the silence of a quiet heart, to the Word Who was God. In the silence of Gethsemane He gave Himself to His Father's will. Jesus was majestically silent before the worldly man who put Him on trial and to torture, accepted the silence of His Father on Golgotha, and in silence of Easter morning conquered the silence of death.

One of the most bizarre occurrences in all of Scripture comes in the apocalyptic writing of the book of Revelation. No other biblical document has suffered more misinterpretation and misapplication of intended meaning than the autograph by John. Its mysterious contents have aroused the attention, excitement, and imagination of readers since its inception.

Depicting events of the end of time as we know it, has produced a Godly fear of standing before the Heavenly Throne and answering for the deeds done in our lives. The final war between good and

Shhh...Listening For God

evil, the Battle of Armageddon, captures the imagination and stirs the conscience. Like screams in the amusement park as the roller coaster plunges down the steep hill, excitement and fear prove difficult to separate.

In the beginning of chapter eight John writes:

When He opened the seventh seal, there was silence in Heaven for about half an hour.

Here we have the last reference of silence in the Bible. Typically we think of eternity with music, choirs, songs, and worship as the angels cry *"Holy, Holy, Holy."* Why this period of silence? Just thirty minutes. It is hard to conceive that the redeemed, the martyred, and the Angelic, will be in total silence, stunned with awe. But they will be. Heaven will be silent, at least for a time.

A moment of silence can be a powerfully moving tribute. How often have we been in a stadium, a school gym, even in church where a time of closed lips is offered as the highest memorial, an accolade, to a life that has passed over to the other shore.

Thirty minutes of silence plays a significant role in the unfolding of the Revelator's visions. I have been to the Isle of Patmos twice and am most humbled to have walked its rocky terrain. I have toured the monastery and cave where John dictated his thoughts to a scribe. Bells still ring out and prayers are offered daily in this isolated spot in the Aegean Sea.

John's seclusion and the simplicity of his surroundings provided him with the spiritual essentials—solitude and silence. By now we

Shhh...Listening For God

know what happened next. *"Deep calleth unto deep."* **In the cell of seclusion, revelation was born. What John heard in private became the shout of eternal proclamation.**

At the opening of the Seventh and final Seal, a breathless silence will descend in anticipation of the judgments of the Scroll being unfolded. Pause has always been instrumental as a communicative device. Total stillness serves in Revelation to deepen the suspense and magnify the hearing of the judgments which are about to fall upon the earth.

Although thirty minutes is a relatively short time, tensions mount in critical moments. Pastorally, I have been with men and women, children and families as we waited in silent apprehension for the doctor's report. We could cut the fear fraught atmosphere with a knife. Habakkuk, Zephaniah, and Zechariah, prophetic voices of old, remind us: *"The LORD is in His Holy Temple; let all the earth be silent before Him."*

Imagine the complete absence of sound. During this interval, trumpets are given to the Angels before the Throne. Meanwhile, another Angel standing by the Altar mingles Heavenly incense with the prayers of the saints. With deliberate action, fire from the Altar is taken, the censer is filled, and cast upon the earth. Judgment has begun.

Silence allows our focus to shift squarely upon God, all that God is and all that God will do. We can hear God in the silence. In silence we distinguish the Spirit's penetrating Voice.

Shhh...Listening For God

George Mueller, whose persistence in petitional prayer is unmatched in the chronicles of intercession, asking God on behalf of others, had a distinctive twist on *Kneeology*. He said, *"The most important time of prayer is the first 15 minutes after you say, Amen."* Have we left our prayer closet too early?

Waiting before the Lord takes patience. Our prayer in all likelihood is a way of emptying us of human thoughts and human speech, after which we are ready to pray prayerfully. Emilee Griffin, in *Clinging: The Experience of Prayer*, masterfully shares:

> All in me is silent, and I am immersed in the silence of God. It is in this stillness that He carries us—it is in the living stillness that we taste of Him Who made us and meant from the beginning that we should belong to Him.

For me, entering this silence was difficult, very difficult. In the past, I would regularly speak and leave my imploring plea at God's feet, then tiptoe away trusting in Heaven's gracious working on my behalf. But I have learned it is in the still, silent dialogue of inner reflection that I discover God's will.

One night in Jerusalem I sat with a tour guide, Joey, whose understanding of archaeology was profound. Several other guests joined us. Dinner conversation was quite mixed, switching time and again from topic to topic; politics, war, ancient ruins, digs and discoveries, news, family, politics, artifacts, terrorism, and back to archaeology.

I really had to pay attention or be lost completely in the shifting sequence. No one really agreed on anything and everyone had a vocalized perspective on something.

My distinguished friend could see the bewilderment in my eyes and graciously said, *"It is all rather Talmudic."* That short phrase has helped me immensely to understand biblical life and the discussions of Jesus, whether with the Pharisees and Sadducees, or sinners and servants. Prayer is Talmudic. It is dialogical, not ceremonial.

I wonder if God withholds our answers simply so that we will come back and continue our relationship with the Divine. At least it is conversation between God and son, God and daughter, or just the sheer joy of sharing the silent presence of another as the Quakers have modeled for us so well.

Prayer in the teachings of Jesus is based on importunity— shameless persistence. The injunctions, *"Ask, and keep on asking, seek and keep on seeking, knock and keep on knocking,"* make perfect sense in the Hebraic understanding of things spiritual. And so does the trusting silence in every relationship which experiences real depth of being.

When the LORD utters, *"Come now, and let us reason together,"* God means it. Abraham, Jacob, Moses, and others display this interactive friendship with the Almighty. Deliberate debate as well as conversational agreement are pertinent to their Divine connection. The Hebrew word for prayer and wrestle is the same.

It proves necessarily difficult to speak and hear at the same time. When we talk, our outer ears are turned off and our inner ears are turned on. We hear ourselves talking, but we do not hear what others are saying.

Shhh...Listening For God

Remember the moment you first heard yourself on a recording device? Here you thought you would sound like someone famous, maybe even tonally appealing. Instead, your voice may have sounded high and squeally, or low and monotone. It is because you heard yourself for the first time with your outer ears. What a shock, eh!?

Prayer is a delicate combination of speech and silence, request and quiet, utterance and reticence. It is conversational. It requires us to attend to the other—our God.

German King, Frederick II, was an influential individual with a thirst for knowledge. In his court he entertained astronomers, mathematicians, scientists, and searched for meaning in a number of ways. He spoke six languages, which led him to a most outlandish experiment.

He wanted to know what the original language of the earth was. Was it Hebrew, Greek, Latin, or some other dialect long forgotten? So he conducted a study with infants. He reasoned that if they were secluded from any verbal influence, no language prejudice, when they finally spoke, it would be the original language of earth.

In the experiment, nurses took infants from their mothers and were instructed not to influence these young babies with any cultural accent. It was surmised that when they were finally able to talk, the babies would speak the original language. But after one year in speechless isolation, all the children died.

We need dialogue, we need it desperately. Conversation is necessary for our physiological and psychological wellness. Silence is just as necessary. Life is always a delicate mixture of dynamics.

Whenever one or the other extends itself beyond appropriate boundaries, consequence is bound to happen.

The Romans had an expression in Latin that said, *"You fatigue the Divine."* We flood God with words, thinking in our *"much speaking,"* we will get an audience with the King. A relationship cannot endure without open, honest, and direct communication. Yet, our souls cannot be sustained without periods of real quietness.

Have you ever fasted? Biblically, we think of a fast as not eating for a period of time, 3 days, 7, 14, or 21 days. An extended fast would be 40 days. But fasts come in different forms. We can fast from shopping, television, the cell phone and computer, or from any other compulsive attraction. Fasting breaks the dependence.

Jesus fasted for over six weeks. Do we realize that Holy Scripture contains no recorded conversations between God and Son within that designated time period? Nor is there any recorded dialogue between Jesus and any other individuals. Was Jesus practicing a verbal fast in order to eliminate other dependencies?

Most Christians live with the misconception that words are more important than silence; that words are more powerful than stillness. As noted, Proverbs, with their tempered blend of mirth and seriousness, link much talkativeness with much sinfulness. That ought to shut us up for a while.

In Youngstown, Ohio there was an Abbot of the Carmelite Order who wanted to know how much speaking Jesus actually did during His earthly ministry. Eliminating obvious Gospel repetitions, he

Shhh...Listening For God

decided to record all the words of the Galilean fisherman he could find in the New Testament, those words in red, and recite them onto a cassette tape recorder.

When he was finished recording, he played back the readings and timed the recitation. Can you take a guess how long it was? Eleven minutes.

This priest was able to read aloud in 660 seconds all the words of Jesus we have. Striking, isn't it? From thirty-three years of Incarnate existence, we have so little Divine speech. Even so, these eleven minutes have changed the world forever.

So what was Jesus doing the rest of the time? Listening. When we speak from silence, we don't have to be long to be strong. *Run Silent, Run Deep.*

Well, what else do I need to say? If I continue, I'll be the undoing of my own project. Above all that I have written, please attend to the mindful phrase *"silence is always a precursor to revelation."*

Do you want to understand more? Do you want to cooperate with God's Spirit in greater measure? Do you want a more intimate fellowship with the Divine?

Then read the writings and listen to the words of those who have gone before you. The path is always the same. Seek solitude. Practice silence. Embrace simplicity. God will unfold within you. The rest will come out through you in your demeanor toward others. Then you will know and the community will see you have been with God.

Shhh...Listening For God

Such endorsement must come through the SSS. If it arrives any other way, pride may infect the glorious outcome of the journey. What a waste. God resists the proud, as unmistakably stated. For pride—a selfish thing—breaks down our relationship with God and others.

However, if the Touch of the Divine Spirit is upon us, silence, solitude, and simplicity will help us stay humble. God, who is mighty and awesome, desires to work through us with gracious acts of love and deliverance, setting free the many who are oppressed in body, mind, or soul.

God's Hand upon us is for more than personal endowment. We are to become extensions of Heaven's grace, conformed into the image of Christ. Thus, we go about doing good, all in Jesus' Name.

Shhh...Listening For God

Listening for God Discussion Questions
<u>Chapter 12 – Run Silent, Run Deep</u>

1. Have you ever considered the monastic way of life? When? Why?

2. Do you feel safer as you go deeper into silence and solitude?

3. How difficult is it for you to keep silent for 30 minutes without a diversion such as reading? Will you try this?

4. How do you feel about Angels?

5. What happens to you when you realize God wants to work through you?

Chapter Thirteen

THE SILENT TREATMENT

Are you an Anti-Dentite? In Sein-Language, Seinfeld that is, it means those fears we face by going to the dentist. Just the sound of the drill *"shivers me timbers."* Give me the laughing gas, the numbing gel, the shots of Novocain, then put me to sleep. Wake me when it's all over.

My annual cleaning, a preventive check-up paid for by the ever-more-costly dental insurance, revealed no real problems. No cavities. No shooting pain from cold water rinses, or jolting aches from tapping on my old silver fillings. *"Does this hurt?"* Got a free toothbrush. Shouldn't that be teethbrush? Whatever.

"Reverend May, you have a small discolored growth on your tongue. It seems to have gotten bigger since your last visit. I'm going to send you to an oral surgeon. This needs to be removed and evaluated immediately."

Fear entered my heart. I have faced fear before, usually with other people. Praying for the sick. Visiting the hospitalized or homebound. It was all different now that it was my own tongue,

199

Shhh...Listening For God

my mouth, my life. A growth, what is it? Where did it come from? Surgeon? That can't be good.

Assuringly, the dentist says, *"Probably nothing."* But it was not his tongue. It was my tongue. I recalled poignantly that a dear friend died from something this small in the same place.

You can well imagine the anxiety that arose. I did my best to *"capture every thought,"* but they were coming rather fast. I quoted my Scriptures of faith and trust, and of healing and provision, but there was a relentless barrage from which even my busyness could not distract.

As one who makes his livelihood from public speaking, I faced a worrisome dilemma. What if? What if I were to lose my tongue? Was I jumping to unrealistic conclusions or processing realistically the unexpected twists and turns of life?

To lose one's tongue may be a blessing in many ways. Calvin Coolidge said *"I have never been hurt by anything I did not say."* Agreed. Many of us have hurt ourselves repeatedly with things we've said, especially when those words boomeranged. My pastor, the late Buddy Harrison, always used to say, *"Keep your words sweet, because one day they may be what you eat."* How true.

As a young boy, I lived in the then rural town of Aurora, Ohio. It was a small neighborly village, friendly and peaceful. Our fourteen acres with a wooded forest for camping and a lake for fishing and summer swimming, designated our place as a local hangout. Three

Shhh...Listening For God

boys, each with several friends, made the May home the place to be on the weekends

"Cleter," my mother's bestowed nickname, untiringly cooked loaf after loaf of French Toast for our Saturday morning breakfast eating contests. She was a gracious lady with Czechoslovakian roots. Cleta Druso was her maiden name.

After school, I would race down our long driveway just in time to watch a favorite cartoon program, *"Rocky and Bullwinkle."* A flying squirrel and a talking moose made for joyful afternoons before homework and dinner. My brother Tom joined in.

Every so often, Rocket J. Squirrel and his antlered sidekick would introduce a short parody. *Aesop's Fables* were a house favorite. Romanesquely garbed characters and goofy plots with sappy moral endings made us laugh, but also made us think. One such tale about the tongue has withstood the passage of time.

In the tale, Xanthus, the heathen philosopher, was entertaining some dinner guests. He sent Aesop to the market to purchase the best victuals he could afford. Aesop returned only with tongue. The cook was ordered to serve tongue with different sauces for every course of the meal. Appetizers—tongue. Salad—tongue. Dinner—tongue.

Our host, Xanthus, was furious. *"Aesop, did I not tell you to buy the best the market offered?"* *"Yes,"* replied Aesop. *"I did as you asked. Is there anything better than tongue? It is the bond of civil society, the organ of truth and reason, and the instrument of our praise to the gods."*

Shhh...Listening For God

Irritated with reddened face, Xanthus ordered Aesop to go back to the market and purchase the worst things he could find. Guess what?

The following evening dinner was served. *"What! tongue again?"* exclaimed Xanthus. *"Most assuredly,"* said Aesop. *"Tongue is most certainly the worst thing in the world. It is the instrument of all strife and contention, the inventor of lawsuits, and the source of division and wars; it is the organ of error, of lies, calumny and blasphemies."*

Tongueless. I could learn to speak with my hands. I could write books. I could sing a song, finally on key. I could pretend I'm deaf and let people speak with unguarded tongues and then respond with pad and pen, like Zacharias.

In the end, I committed my journey to the Almighty. God's *"all things"* plan works. It just doesn't always work the way I think it should. That's why God is God and I remain a trusting son in need of healing grace. *"All things do work together for good."* I realize now that I do not get to decide what is the *"good"* or when. God does. God is the *Great Physician.*

In the book *Hinds Feet On High Places* by British missionary, Hannah Hurnard, a question is directed from the Lord to the main character of her autograph. *"Much-Afraid, don't you know by now that I never think of you as you are now but as you will be when I have brought you from all the stains and defilements of the journey?"*

Shhh...Listening For God

My mother developed cancer when I was young. Back then, it was a new term. No chemo treatment. Remove the breast. Fortunately, she lived a long healthy life without any recurrence. I thought of her as I lay back in the surgeon's elongated black leather chair. An automatic blood pressure machine rang out in warning. I had exceeded the limit. Do I get a ticket for racing too fast? The procedure hadn't even started. What next?

"You won't feel much but a little prick." My oral surgeon had great bedside manners. He was both talkative and sensitive. After numbing the tongue with a cotton swab, he readied his needle with what was supposed to keep me from feeling pain. With gauze he gripped my pinkish budded taster and in one guided motion pulled with a squeeze. He injected several times a piercing, burning fluid into the tip of my nervously extended saliva coated muscle. *"Almost done."*

The laser biopsy was over. Stitches were in with directions to suck on popsicles and not use a straw to drink cold soothing milkshakes. Use a spoon. *"Fill these prescriptions, you're going to need them."*

Then I waited. I'm not sure which was worse; the surgical ordeal or the not knowing. Time, was it my friend or my enemy? I found myself trying to practice my own preaching. Have faith. I rehearsed my tonguelessness just in case, *"The pen is mightier than the sword."*

I am learning to be silent, keeping my mouth shut. Surgically it may be forced upon me. So be it. I am out of options. What's the message here Lord?

> Tyre and Sidon. And behold, a woman of Canaan came from that region and cried out to Him, saying, "Have mercy on me, O Lord, Son of David! My daughter is severely demon-possessed." **But He answered her not a word.** And His disciples came and urged Him, saying, "Send her away, for she cries out after us."
>
> Matthew 15:21-23

Ruth Graham, the Reverend Billy Graham's wife, stated at a conference; *"God has not always answered my prayers. If He had, I would have married the wrong man several times."* Me? I am glad some of my supplications have gone without immediate responses. We do not always know what is best for us.

Jesus retreated into the coastal region of Tyre and Sidon, about 20 miles west over the mountains from the Galilee. The Syro-Phoenician woman of the story was a descendant of the ancient Canaanite race, which was a notorious enemy of the Jews, as noted by the historian, Josephus. The Canaanite cities of Tyre and Sidon represented the most extreme kind of paganism that a Jew in Jesus' day could expect to encounter.

When the Canaanites were driven out of the Land, they finally inhabited the coasts of the Mediterranean and became dwellers by the sea. They were the first to make use of an alphabet, and all modern lettered nomenclature can be attributed to this early people.

Jesus' perceived rude silence was, at first glance, offensive. Sure, I've been tired by the pressing needs of people, but not to speak anything, an excuse, an explanation is a bit much for someone who is termed to be "no respecter of someone's person." What's the deal *Schlemiel*?

Could it be that Jesus used silence not as a repellent, but as an attractant, something to draw her ever closer? His tightlipped stance ultimately pulled from her the faith required to achieve her desired miracle, a prayer, I might add, not for self but for another. In this case, the means were justified by the end. Her daughter was made well.

> Then Jesus answered and said to her, "O woman, great *is* your faith! Let it be to you as you desire." And her daughter was healed from that very hour.

Silence is effective. **Like a magnet which extracts the necessary elements from crowded surroundings, silence pulls from the heart of our beings virtuous awareness of God in Divine fullness.** Silence in self should take us to places of peaceful rest in Eternal Presence. And silence from Eternal Presence should take us back into a more trusting self. Either way, spirituality is in play.

In this spiritual context, listening is the central element of silence, a dynamic Christians cannot live without. Many factors like maturity and ministry all grow from this basic principle, which so often is the neglected foundation.

"I don't have time" is a repeated phrase which must be challenged. We let the world dictate the pace of life and the cost is much, much too high.

The University of Minnesota did a study which discovered that 60% of all business misunderstandings were a result of poor listening. How we hear affects everything we do and eventually who we become. It was that way for me.

In my life as a young Catholic, the Church Calendar contained special seasons and days for many reasons. As an altar boy who prayed the old Latin prayers, rang bells appropriately, and attended to the priestly functions, I learned about Liturgical incorporations into the yearly movements. As the seasonal calendar moved from month to month, so also did the Church Calendar.

Have you ever heard of *Ember Days?* Ember is a term representative of the four seasons, not the singing group mind you, but fall, winter, spring, and summer. Literally, *Ember Days* were just that, days to catch up and stoke the coals and stir the embers of spiritual renewal in our lives.

The early church saw the need for maintaining proper periods of rest. Renewal comes only when we stop long enough for listening and for weaving what we have learned into the fabric of our lives.

What sleep is to the body, silence is to the soul. How long can we continue without sleep? Not very long before we collapse. A tired driver is just as dangerous as a drunk driver, if not more so.

Shhh...Listening For God

When we are tired, our thoughts are clouded, and our decisions are poor. We need rest.

We are MADD at the alcoholized, but what about the omitted practice of silent listening? Shouldn't we be just as MAD at allowing our lives to proceed at breakneck speed, maybe even putting passengers at risk, and not slowing down to stop, look, and listen? *Selah* is just another poetic vocab, no longer a psalmistic expression of rest. Could God's silence in our lives be a Heavenly instrument drawing us ever closer to Divine Presence?

Ember Days occur in clusters, Wednesday, Friday, Saturday, four times a year; one cluster for each season. Historically, they arrive after the First Sunday of Lent, after Pentecost Sunday, in autumn after Holy Cross Day, and after the Third Sunday of Advent.

These *Ember Days* are days of prayer, rest, silence, and fasting, meant to restore the human soul with renewed strength. They are derived from the Latin *Quatuor Temporum*, the beginning of the Four Seasons. Have you had Shrimp Tempura at your favorite restaurant? A Portuguese Missionary came up with the tasty recipe as a meatless dish to be enjoyed during an *Ember Day* fast.

Zechariah speaks of four fasts which may have influenced the Christian application of these designated times. Regardless, from the earliest of records, biblical and otherwise, fasts were instituted in the lives of God's people for intentional purposes. These times brought the restoration of life.

Shhh...Listening For God

The tempo of time will never slow down. We must take time, prayer time, silent time, to be with the God who cares. Hopefully we care enough about ourselves and the God who loves us to share time, space, and place.

Seconds, minutes, and hours are the most expensive commodity we have. I know of no greater gift than day or date. Its value far exceeds pre-written cards and pre-packaged presents. Let us give ourselves and others the gift that keeps on giving. Time. Give God the gift that keeps us listening. Silence. God will respond.

Well. The doctor called. *"I have an update on your biopsy."* *"Yes?"* I sat on the edge of my bed. Seconds ticked loudly, my heart beating through my chest. *"Everything is okay."*

My experience had been epiphanous to say the least. How many others have had to face much worse? Speech is precious. The organ of utterance was once a taken-for-granted member of the anthropological wonder called the human body. Not anymore. Even the possibility of enforced silence has changed my heart.

Friends were supportive, and most importantly, prayerful. Their tender checking-in at various points in my waiting proved valuable as I moved through the demands of each ensuing day. Thank you.

I am humbled by the choice to speak or not to speak. Both will be forever honored. But I am learning that deeper listening brings exclamatory life. I am committed to the journey of deeper life.

Shhh...Listening For God

If I am to communicate words with power, verbiage with punch, it will come only when sentences stitched together form paragraphs of deeper meaning, which have matured in seasons of secluded silence.

Shhh...Listening For God

Listening for God Discussion Questions
Chapter 13 – The Silent Treatment

1. Have you experienced the fear of a prognosis that leaves you waiting for an answer? How did you react, immediately, and after some time elapsed?

2. Do you agree that silence is the rest for the soul? When did you last try it?

3. How did you feel when you experienced the deep beyond deep? Did God meet you there?

4. Can you describe how silence can be refreshment for the soul?

5. Why does it take courage and patience to encounter the Great Mystery in silence?

Epilogue

DO YOU HEAR WHAT I HEAR?

As Ruth Haley Barton has said, *"Truth be told, it was desperation that first propelled me into solitude and silence."* Maybe it's that way for many of us. I'd rather have listening for God be derived from a passionate desire than a desperate search. But who of us hasn't looked up when we were down, or listened in when all other voices speaking out were cryptically hopeless.

Have you heard God's Voice recently? Jesus didn't passively wait. He actively engaged with God, and most frequently in seclusion.

Now in the morning, having risen a long while before daylight, He went out and departed to a solitary place; and there He prayed.

This Markan writing is provoking when we consider that his Gospel was written based on Peter's reflections. Jesus actually did what the text says He did. Peter was possibly awakened by the rustling motions of Jesus rising and departing from the dimly glowing coals of the campsite to wander off somewhere in the misty dew of dawn.

Shhh...Listening For God

Seclusion, even for Jesus, was not easy to come by. When the disciples discovered His morning disappearance they *"followed after Him."* The picture in the Greek is a little more intense. They *"hunted"* for Him. Disruptions come, most often from those closest to us. But hold fast. **Breakaway is the path to breakthrough.**

On the surface, praying early in the morning may not seem all that peculiar. But the Jewish day begins at dusk not dawn. Nicodemus came to visit Jesus at night. Were his nightfall movements statements of trepidation; was he trying to protect his reputation from other Pharisees and Scribes? Seemingly, he was just doing his usual evening rounds of priestly touch points. Nothing secretive, but so, so inquisitive.

In the Genesis account, *"The evening and the morning"* cycle was the paradigm of time. However, the long-standing model of the created order changes as the New Testament demonstrates a unique inversion. *"In the end of Sabbath, as it began to dawn toward the first day of the week. . ."* something dramatic occurs. RESURRECTION.

Early morning now belongs to the Church of the Risen Christ. As He ascends, the Spirit of Pentecost descends in the third hour of the day, nine o'clock, a.m.

Do you hear what I hear? A new faith is birthed at a new time for a new people. We are *"Children of the Day."* As Paul proclaims, Jew and Gentile have become one. Not only are we new creatures, creation itself sighs in expectant anticipation of the earnest, the down payment of what is to come at the end of it all. No night, just the Light of God's countenance. In Christian eschatology, eternity has begun.

But for now, health concerns are being expressed by socio-religious thinkers regarding the homogenization of the hours. Day and night, for the most part, are no longer distinguishable. Labor and leisure dangerously move *a mile a minute* into one long, quickened period of worldly activity.

At the break of dawn, we plunge into the temporal world of things. We come home after overly rigorous work only to enter the computer world of unceasing enticements, virtual friends, and further cyber employment obligations. *Digiholics. Media addicts.* We are caught in the web. *"Overdone good and faithful servant."* Without intervention, there is no way out.

"Where did I meet God today?" is the recurring question of inner accountability. We need to position ourselves before the One and Only whose Voice we long to hear. Prayer determines the quality of each day. Our first silence, our first thoughts, our first words, our first actions belong to the LORD.

My purpose in writing is to provide for us who seek the Voice of voices, some inspirational passages and spiritual guidance in listening for God. Listening leads to devoted affection and fruitful living. This is not always easy, or quick, but in proverbial thought, *practice makes better.*

Practice God's Presence. Implement some spiritual exercises which ready you for Divine interaction. Be silent. Be attentive. Be expectant. You will hear clearly. I'm sure of it. Scripture records, *"You shall call upon Me, and I will answer. . ."* *Shhh.* . . It's time to let God speak.

Appendix

Contemplations for Daily Renewal

Not as though I had already attained, either were already perfect; but I follow after, if that I may apprehend that for which also I am apprehended of Christ Jesus. Brethren, I count not myself to have apprehended; but this one thing I do, forgetting those things which are behind, and reaching forth unto those things which are before, I press toward the mark for the prize of the high calling of God in Christ Jesus. Philippians 3:12-14 KJV

Observation: Forgetting would be easy if some hurts weren't so unforgettable. Like you, I have tried to put some emotional wounds and personal injuries at the foot of the Cross. From there I tuck them seemingly safely away in the quarantined recesses of my mind. Yet every so often, like a water stain that slowly and shamelessly seeps through causing unsightly discoloration, my prior scarring returns in all its raving sensitivity. Our personalities are created in such a way, that no number of spiritual layers can suppress what will need God's healing touch. Trying to forget the unforgettable is an impossible task. We can run, but we can't hide. We can ignore, even deny, but we cannot annul, at least not without consequences, some of which may be far more damaging than the initial event.

It has been said and bears repeating, "The mind is a wonderful thing. It starts working the minute you are born and doesn't stop until you stand up to speak in public." For those of us who address the masses, we identify with this observation. Even so, our internal computers are quite amazing, remembering facts and figures long obsolete. How does the human brain do this? By recalling significant episodes, information, and repetitional patterns.

Eliminating a negative episode in life is highly unlikely, if not nearly impossible. Nonetheless, we can replace it with something positive, something good, something better. It helps to create a hopeful outlook of the

Shhh...Listening For God

future. Rather than being held captive by former pain, fresh, positive experiences offer healthy release by overcoming evil with good.

So when Paul writes "forgetting those things which are behind," what exactly is he getting at? If anyone had things to forget, it was Paul. As chief among sinners and persecutor *par excellence,* Paul's former actions could stir up a host of deep seated emotions—guilt, shame, condemnation, and all self-applied. When he made "havoc" in the Church, it is an image of a wild boar ripping up a vineyard. Like the Apostle, I long to press toward the mark of the high calling of God in Christ Jesus. But my past acts are like weights around my ankles making it ever more difficult to forge ahead. What am I to do?

Interpretation: Although stated in three verses, Paul's balanced presentation appears in just two short sentences, each very similar. For both have "I press on" (*dioko*) as the main verb, followed by an important disclaimer "I have not arrived," and then a statement about what he is pressing toward. The only notable distinction between the two is the addition of "forgetting [disregarding] what lies behind." Paul's admission that he has "not already attained" may seem a simple matter of apostolic humility. Or, he is pointing out what is yet to come. He is certainly emphasizing the pursuit of his goal (the last point in each sentence), however, he equally stresses that he has not achieved that goal. Other congregations in the early church had become fascinated with spiritual perfection, a form of maturity, which believes "since I have arrived, everything is permissible." Thus, ethical behavior waned. Paul is intent to not let his language be misinterpreted, especially with Gnostic overtones of super-spirituality and the perfectionism associated with the initiation rites of the mystery religions. Paul affirms the incompleteness of his own journey and like everyone else, awaits that final day. In the meantime, he presses on, an expression used in athletics and war showing intense commitment and determination. The Philippian believers are to follow his example. Don't get distracted by looking back. Look forward. From the opening verses of this letter (1:25 and following), Paul expresses his concern regarding their progress in the faith.

As a runner, Paul pays no attention to the things that are behind. Given the conflict with the Judaizers who were requiring New Testament believers to strictly follow the Mosaic Law, the Apostle is, with slight of hand, challenging this Gospel distortion. If the Philippians considered the return to Torah observance as advancement, they would be pressing toward the

Shhh...Listening For God

very thing Paul left behind, moreover, what he considers "refuse." So what exactly are we to forget? "Forgetting" (*epilanthanomenos*) speaks of something different than our English understanding of the term. Typically, we interpret forgetting as obliterating some instance from our memories. *Epilanthanomenos*, however, implies a continual process in contrast to a one-time occurrence. And it demonstrates the necessity of pushing something out of the mind. Some scholars translate it "to disregard, or to neglect", showing a nagging distraction and the constant need to deal with it, putting it in its rightful place.

Paul's point of discussion is his progress as a believer. Elsewhere when he uses athletic imagery, his focus is on his labor in the Kingdom. Such is the case here as well. The point? Paul does not rest on his accomplishments or successes of the past. He keeps looking forward, straining, pressing and pursuing until that day when he, and we, shall be presented blameless to Christ (I Thess. 3:13; 5:23). What he is "disregarding" are his past triumphs and resulting profits (3:7), not his failures, setbacks, and afflictions. Resting on our laurels can be just as debilitating as languishing over our rejections. Christ is all and in all. And to win Christ is everything.

Application: This passage is compelling. We lost our favorite method to deal with pain, that is, to try to forget about it. Rather than bury the past, God can use personal hurts to build a future. Alcoholics Anonymous has a slogan that seems fitting: "Close the door of your past, but be sure it's a glass door." In other words, don't allow your past hurts to control you presently, but, as well, don't forget the pain from which God has delivered you. I believe we need to get in touch with our *woundedness* and allow God to take what was meant for evil and use it for good. It is not hard to discover personal conflicts. Get quiet. Ask the Holy Spirit to search your inner life. Wait. And listen. Then follow God's prescription.

What about our accomplishments? Counting everything as loss to find Christ is more challenging than lifting our wounds to Him. We must be willing to let go of everything to press toward maturity in Christ. Paul's example may very well tell us it is not our troubles, but our triumphs that keep us from moving on in our journey toward God. Anything holding you back? Press on, dear friend, press on. You will sense God's embrace. Promise.

SELECTED BIBLIOGRAPHY

Barton, Ruth Haley. *Invitation to Solitude and Silence, Experiencing God's Transforming Presence*. Downers Grove, IL: InterVarsity Press, 2004.

Browning, Elizabeth Barrett. *The Oxford Book of Mystical English Verse*. Nicholson & Lee, Eds., 1917.

Case, E. Max. *A Modern Adaptation of a Fairy Tale: The Wolf as Teacher*. This is an unpublished manuscript.

Diamond, John. *Your Body Doesn't Lie*. New York, NY: Grand Central Publishing, 1989.

Dossey, Larry. *Space, Time & Medicine*. Boston, MA: Shambhala Publishing, Inc., 1982.

Easton, Matthew G. *The Bible Dictionary: Your Biblical Reference Book*. Charleston, SC: Forgotten Books, 2007.

Griffin, Emilee. *Clinging: The Experience of Prayer*. New York, NY: McCracken Press, 1994.

Gungor, Ed. *Religiously Transmitted Diseases*. Nashville, TN: Nelson Books, 2006.

Hall, Sister Jeremy. *Silence, Solitude, Simplicity, A Hermit's Love Affair with a Noisy, Crowded, and Complicated World.* Collegeville, MN: Liturgical Press, 2007.

Hemfelt, Robert, Minirth, Frank, Meier, Paul. *We Are Driven: The Compulsive Behaviors America Applauds.* Nashville, TN: Thomas Nelson Publishers, 1991.

Hurnard, Hannah. *Hinds' Feet On High Places.* Wheaton, IL: Tyndale House, 1988.

Kelly, Thomas R. *The Testament of Devotion.* New York, NY: Harper-Collins Publishers, Inc., 1996.

Lewis, C.S. *The Screwtape Letters.* New York, NY: Harper-Collins Publishers, 2001.

Lloyd, Seth. *Programming the Universe.* New York, NY: Random House, Inc., 2006.

Lucado, Max. *Applause of Heaven.* Nashville, TN: Thomas Nelson, 1999.

May, Gerald. *Dark Night of the Soul.* New York, NY: Harper-Collins Publishers, 2005.

Norris, Gunilla. *Inviting Silence, Universal Principles of Meditation.* New York, NY: BlueBridge, 2004.

Norris, Kathleen. Quoted from, *Silence, Solitude, Simplicity* by Sister Jeremy Hall. Collegeville, MN: Liturgical Press, 2007.

Nouwen, Henri. *The Way of the Heart.* New York, NY: HarperOne, 1991.

Pearsall, Paul, Ph.D. *Making Miracles.* New York, NY: Prentice Hall Press, 1991.

Schwartz, Gary E. R., and Russek Linda G.S Russek. *The Living Universe: A Fundamental Discovery that transforms Science & Medicine*. Charlottesville, VA: Hampton Roads Publishing Co., Inc., 1999.

Shaw, Lynda Rebecca. *As Promised*. Http://www.Myspace.com/ LyndaRebeccaShaw, (14, July, 2011).

Skinner, Stephen. *Sacred Geometry, Deciphering the Code*. New York, NY: Sterling Publishing Co., Inc., 2006.

Smith, Jami. *Wash Over Me*. Mobile, AL: Hosanna/Vertical Music, 2002.

Steindl-Rast, David and Lebell, Sharon. *Music of Silence, A Sacred Journey Through the Hours of the Day*. Berkley, CA: Harper Collins Publishers, 1998.

Steere, Douglas. *On Listening to Another*. New York, NY: Harper & Bros., 1955.

Tomlin, Chris. *How Great is Our God*. Roswell, GA: Six Steps Records, 2004.

Willard, Dallas. *The Spirit of The Disciplines, Understanding How God Changes Lives*. New York, NY: Harper Collins Publishers, 1991.

BOOK ENDORSEMENTS:

"Israel: A Biblical Tour of the Holy Land *is one of the finest introductory works I have discovered. It is comprehensive in its scope but non-technical in its descriptions and illustrations.*

This work could be of great benefit to persons contemplating making a tour of the Holy Land as well as for persons who have already traveled there and who need to review what they saw. The work could also be of great benefit to study groups in schools and churches who are seeking further background material on the life and times of the Bible. This work is readable, portable, and attractively presented."

Dr. O. Kenneth Walther,
Professor of Greek and New Testament

"*During my twenty years of guiding pilgrims in the Holy Land, I have read literally hundreds of books on the sites of this country. In Dr. May's book I found a thoughtful and fascinating blend of history, Bible, archaeology, and current events. I am confident that for my professional colleagues, this book will rank second only to the Bible as a source-book for the Holy Land. And the pilgrim or tourist to Israel will find that* Israel: A Biblical Tour of the Holy Land *will round out his or her experience and make it that much more perfect.*"

Benji Shavit, Tour Guide

ALSO AVAILABLE:

ISRAEL
A Biblical Tour of the Holy Land

After visiting Israel, many people understand why it is called the "Fifth Gospel." Just as the four Gospels of the New Testament portray a different face of Jesus' life and ministry, the land and culture of Israel bring revelation and added dimension to His humanity, divinity, and teachings. In *Israel: A Biblical Tour of the Holy Land* you will:

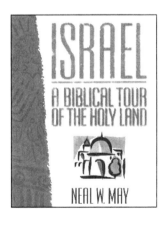

- Walk the streets Jesus walked
- Visit the homes of biblical prophets
- Gain insights into ancient mysteries
- Unlock well-loved passages of the Bible

Please join us as we visit the Land where Heaven touches Earth.

ALSO AVAILABLE:

Me or We?
Discovering the Power of Biblical Community

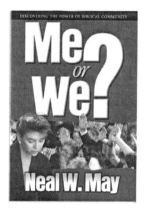

All fields of science have proven that partnership begets wellness. It is the very heartbeat of the universe. Even atomic particles travel in pairs. Whether we speak of emotional, physical, or spiritual health, wellness is always spelled with a "we." In the biblical sense we call it unity.

The Bible begins with the plurality of God. Everything we read and everything we experience thereafter reflects this covenantal relationship within the Godhead. The plague of individualism begins early in the Bible as well. Into this very world of selfishness God sends His message of community. While other world religions stress individual purity, Christianity puts its emphasis on corporate togetherness.

Call it what you like, agreement more than moves the hand of God, it manifests God's Presence in our midst. This is how we conquer. No wonder "two are better than one." Rather than forsake God's plan for us as the family of God, we need to gather once again in celebration of our calling.

BOOK ENDORSEMENTS:

"This book is a tool. It drilled a pilot hole in our autonomous hearts and opened our lives to the convicting truth of Scripture, allowing the transforming power of the Holy Spirit to begin. Our small group's perception of community has been dramatically changed."

Dave DeCrane, Westerville, OH

"When Pastor May released this book, I read it and immediately ordered copies for all my church leaders. The focus on our need for 'we-ism' is precisely what the church community requires today. I have used the book as a text for cell meetings, and took each chapter as a topic for our weekly gatherings. Our small group discussions were very positive and provoked our church to focus on the corporate rather than the individual."

Dan Pavlansky, Pastor
Faith Fellowship Church
Yadkinville, North Carolina

CPSIA information can be obtained at www.ICGtesting.com
Printed in the USA
BVOW072344200312

285667BV00002B/3/P